THE
FORMULA
FOR
SUCCESS

THE
FORMULA
FOR
SUCCESS

HOW TO WIN AT LIFE
USING YOUR OWN
PERSONAL ALGORITHM

SAMUEL LEACH

CAPSTONE
A Wiley Brand

This edition first published 2019

© 2019 Samuel Leach

Registered office

John Wiley & Sons Ltd, The Atrium, Southern Gate, Chichester, West Sussex, PO19 8SQ, United Kingdom

For details of our global editorial offices, for customer services and for information about how to apply for permission to reuse the copyright material in this book please see our website at www.wiley.com.

Library of Congress Cataloging-in-Publication Data is Available.

ISBN 9780857088222 (paperback)
ISBN 9780857088192 (ePDF)
ISBN 9780857088215 (ePub)

Cover Design: Wiley

Set in 12/16pt, NewBaskervilleStd by SPi Global, Chennai, India.

Printed in Great Britain by TJ International Ltd, Padstow, Cornwall, UK

10 9 8 7 6 5 4 3 2 1

Contents

Introduction

Life is a puzzle that the greatest minds on earth have been debating, theorising, and seeking to answer for many thousands of years. From microbes to constellations, the philosophical to the spiritual, and more recently the mysteries of quantum theory and the multiverse, the key to understanding life lies in learning to recognize and work within its patterns and rules. And it is only when you understand the mechanics of any system (including life), that you can begin to truly prosper within its boundaries.

For me, unlocking the prosperity of life is a personal quest that concludes with me being the best that I can be every single day that I draw breath. This book is about the patterns that I've discovered by studying the lives of incredible people, aligning them with my own experiences, and applying those rules to everything that I do. More importantly, it is about how you (whoever you are) can learn to do the same. I dare you to read on and I'll prove it to you.

But if you think that this is just a get-rich-quick scheme, or what I'll be talking to you about will be easy – go and find another book. Because for this to work in your life, for the algorithm to lead you to a life full of wealth and prosperity, you will need to be prepared to get uncomfortable. Massively and seat-squirmingly uncomfortable.

The algorithm of prosperity contained in this book is a series of rules and attitudes which, when uploaded to an open mind, can create as much success as that mind can imagine. If I can do it, starting from a one-bedroom flat which I shared with my Dad and my older brother, so can you. It would be easy to assume that my story revolves around gambling on the stock exchange and getting lucky, or that I started out with my family's financial backing. But you would be wrong on both counts. It involves risk-taking but, as you will discover, there is a gulf between gambling and taking risks; and between getting lucky and the sure-fire algorithm of prosperity,

My success has been built entirely upon attitude and application – trading was merely the road I found myself on. I honestly believe that I would have found the same level of success on any path I had chosen to walk down because I desired it more than anyone else who I encountered. It might have been working on an oil rig, tenpin bowling, being an Xbox champion, boxing, or long-distance swimming. Whatever it was, I believe I would have mastered it. And as for my parents' backing – I had that 100%, but not from their bank accounts; their backing came in the shape of imparting belief and giving me their unconditional love.

Trading has, of course, played a massive part in my life and I will touch on some aspects of it (as a commercial opportunity and as a life skill) as we proceed through the book.

> *'The most dangerous risk of all is the risk of spending your life not doing what you want on the bet that you can buy yourself the freedom to do it later.'*
>
> Alan Watts

What is an algorithm?

Algorithms are the invisible mechanics behind everything you see around you. They are the intricacies of the miracle that turns a seed into a tree, the rules that blend single notes into beautiful harmonics, and the way Google decides what to put at the top of the list when you are searching, researching, buying, or browsing ...

In its simplest form, an algorithm is a mathematical equation which translates input data into a result. Algorithms are both naturally occurring (in that they describe observable behaviours), and intelligently designed (where they can be used to predict outcomes and calculate probabilities). Pretty much everything that you do or connect with each day is based on some sort of algorithm. Let me show you what I mean.

The alarm that woke you up this morning went off because you programmed some pre determined numbers into an electronic device which counts seconds, minutes, and hours. The breakfast that you ate was based on data that you had previously gathered (derived from preferred taste or nutritional values) and the subsequent calculations and decisions you made as a result of that data. The route you took to school or work was not a random journey – it was chosen because you applied an algorithm of convenience, cost, speed, and direction to establish the most appropriate method to get you to where you needed to be. You can apply this thinking to the clothes you are wearing right now, the time of day that you feel most alive, the things you watch on YouTube, the people you spend most of your time with, and the amount of money that sits in your bank account. Whether you are aware of it or not, algorithms control everything that you do. And knowing that simple fact should give you a sense of great power – because it means that different data will generate a different result, and therefore you can change your life.

Even the things that you are currently trying to think of to prove me wrong are algorithms – including all of the random behaviours and circumstances that are outside yours or anybody else's control. You were born into an algorithm based on the genes and circumstances of your parents, the country and location you grew up in, the school you went to, and the tastes that you developed as a child. All these things – in essence, the cultures that surround each one of us – contain the algorithms which shape our lives; or, in other, words the algorithms of life and prosperity.

And, if you still doubt that you are subject to unseen rules that you follow without even thinking, try these tests:

- **Input:** Reach out your hand to someone when you first meet them. **Outcome:** they will reach back and shake your hand.

- **Input:** The next time two or three things go wrong in a row, say to someone, 'it never rains but it …' and stop. **Outcome:** see if they say 'pours' (and probably follow that up with 'tell me about it').

- **Input:** Walk into an lift and face the rear wall. **Outcome:** notice the strange looks – because convention (the algorithm) says that you must face the door in an lift.

- **Input:** When an unfortunate incident is being discussed, make a point of stating that you are sure it would never happen to you. **Outcome:** then watch as within a few moments someone will be looking for a piece of wood to touch and verbalise.

- **Input:** Sit in a different way to everyone else during a meeting (i.e. folded arms, leaning forward or crossing one leg). **Outcome:** notice how, one by one, people around the room will start to imitate your posture.

- **Input:** Close your eyes and do not, whatever you do, think about bananas. **Outcome:** I know what you are thinking!

We are influenced by algorithms and unseen rules all day long. Hopefully, throughout this book, you will start to see how you can change your life by learning and manipulating the rules of the world that surrounds you.

Why do algorithms matter?

If you imagine that everything in life is subject to a set of rules (as described above), and the outcome of that thing is determined by the data which is entered into that set of rules, then it should be possible to predict anything and everything. Now, even all the combined computing power in the world would not be enough to calculate every single potential deciding factor in every situation, but in theory it should be possible.

You are probably thinking now how it might be possible to predict the lottery numbers, the football results each week, or maybe even the rises and falls of the stock exchange. Well, with enough data and a strong enough understanding of the algorithms of probability, research, and proven mathematics, the last of those three (at least) is a genuine opportunity. In my business, as a trader on the stock market and foreign currency exchanges, I apply algorithms to try to predict outcomes. It is not a perfect science, because there are too many variables and rarely enough proven data, but it is reliable enough to build a multi millionaire lifestyle. I don't say that to show off, but because it is both true and eminently possible for anyone.

More importantly than the financial wealth that understanding the mechanics and rules of trading can deliver, however, is the fact that understanding algorithms can be applied to bring prosperity to every area of your life. In the same way that your food choices, travel plans, and entertainment preferences are determined by rules and data that you control, so is everything else. If you apply yourself to understanding these algorithms and you proactively seek to input better data and make smarter decisions, you can have more control over your mindset, your will power, your health, your happiness, and your ability to determine your future prosperity.

In this book, I am going to take you through various times in my own life that I have encountered difficulties and opportunities, and how working out the algorithm helped me succeed. I cannot guarantee that your algorithms will be the same, although I suspect many will be similar, but I hope to show you that there is always a way out and always a way to get up. I will also show you several proven algorithms for creating a more prosperous and wealthy lifestyle. I will share some of the secrets behind my trading success and the approach to life that has brought me to where I am today.

I am not offering an easy-life pill or a get-rich-quick scheme (as I don't believe those things exist) so, if you are looking for something like that, I suggest you stop reading now. I have discovered, studied, and written hundreds of algorithms for all sorts of scenarios, and if there is one thing that is common to every successful algorithm it is the application of effort. Being successful in life is always subject to how much you want it and how hard you are prepared to work for it, but I can promise you one thing – the rewards always far outweigh the effort if you have worked out the correct algorithm.

Algorithms matter because, once you understand that they are rules and you can control them, you can start to control what happens in your life. You can start to activate and cultivate the algorithm of prosperity that will take you to the places that you want to be and help you live the life you want to live.

How to get the most from this book

In this book I will be sharing my experiences: from my childhood and schooldays to finding my way in the trading world and challenging myself to become the best version of me. I know that I'm young (in the eyes of some readers) and still have a lot to learn about life (and I certainly don't want to patronise anybody), but I am also aware that very few people have achieved what I have while still in their 20s. I don't mean to boast; I just want to get your attention in the hope that you take hold of what I have learned so far. And I know that it works because I have seen it change the lives of thousands of people (of all ages) all over the world. Within the pages of this book you will get to meet some of them and hear how the algorithm of life has helped them.

So, even if you don't identify with my story, maybe you will see yourself in some of the people who have become my friends, students, and colleagues along the way. And maybe, just maybe, their stories will change yours.

THE
FORMULA
FOR
SUCCESS

'Fear and greed are the two main reasons that people fail as traders.'

Chapter 1

MIND OVER MONEY

It is easy to imagine that there is a finite amount of money in the world – which is why people believe that one person getting richer means someone else getting poorer. If that were the case, the only way to truly break out of the circumstances into which you were born would be to steal wealth from other people. But the reality is that money is just an invention of humanity which has evolved, expanded, and been governed by a multitude of ever-changing rules throughout the millennia and across many civilisations. Money has always been, and will continue to be, created to fill the needs of commerce. That means that if everyone were more financially intelligent, there would be enough wealth for us all – only you are stopping yourself from prospering.

You could, therefore, conclude that money is no more than a concept, numbers on a computer screen, or a virtual reality game whose rules we have all promised to obey. Today, I have learned to treat money as a game. I don't mean that flippantly or that I don't respect and value what it represents, just that I understand exactly what money is and how it works. And I also like winning games.

So, before I share with you some of the stories and experiences which led me to my conclusions and helped me discover the algorithm of prosperity, I need you to understand a few basic rules. You might like to call these my four top tips for being a successful trader, or a master of money management.

Interestingly, however, only one of the biggest lessons I share with people when they ask me about trading is actually about trading. The real key to financial prosperity is managing the way that you think.

1. Mindset is fundamental

Most people are familiar with the Pareto Principle, also known as the 80:20 Law. It states that in many life scenarios, 80% of the outcomes are a result of 20% of the inputs. For example, people wear 20% of the contents of their wardrobe, 80% of the time; 80% of a company's sales come from 20% of its customers; 20% of the world's population owns 80% of its wealth; 20% of the words in any given language are used 80% of the time, and so on.

Of course, the Pareto Principle is not an exact science (hence calling it a principle), but it is usually a good starting measure in most cases. In trading and wealth management, it is often said that 80% of the art comes down to mindset and 20% the technical skill of knowing how to trade. It is often said – but, as with most things that people say, few actually believe it or choose to put mindset mastery above that of money skill.

I would even go as far as to say that, if you skip through this book looking for the technical tips and insider secrets, you are proving your mindset to be in the 20% and that is why you will never quite achieve your goals. The fact is that if you master the right mindset towards money (give 80% of your time and effort to it), you will definitely reap the benefits faster than those who don't.

Fear and greed

Warren Buffett, possibly the most successful investor of all time, famously said: 'Be fearful when others are greedy and greedy only when others are fearful.' I love this quote (and I can't promise I won't use it again before you finish reading this book) because it is a foundation principle any trader needs to learn. But you don't just need to learn this principle; you need to be able to pull it out of your knowledge and stand on it when the emotions start to kick in – that is why mindset matters.

Knowing that the right thing to do is stay in a trade when everyone else is panicking – or pull out when the rest of the world is dreaming how to spend the profits they haven't made yet – is different to actually doing it. It takes guts, composure, and faith in your previous (hopefully in-depth and diligent) analysis and research.

The reason most people get into trading is that they think it might be an easy way to make a lot of money. As you will learn over the next few chapters, I was one of those people in the beginning. What I learned very quickly, however, was that while it could be a way to make a lot of money, it is far from easy. The other thing I learned was that most other people hadn't clocked onto the 'hard work' aspect of the algorithm – so their loss was my opportunity for gain.

Fear and greed are the two main reasons that people fail as traders. These are mindset issues that need to be fixed before you can move on to dealing with the third problem, which is a technical one. Inexperienced, and to be fair sometimes experienced, traders will always lack patience or panic and pull out too early. The signs are there, the numbers, the patterns, and the algorithms are clearly telling them what will happen next, but their emotions overcome and overwhelm their good judgement.

The biggest practical tip I can share with you here, as you are learning to control your emotions, is very simple: never risk any capital that you cannot afford to lose. If you need to win on any particular deal, as opposed to simply wanting to (and you should always want to), then you make an emotional attachment to the outcome. And the bottom line is that most people without money form a very strong emotional attachment to it. Those who have access to and understand money see it as numbers on a piece of paper or computer screen.

When you learn to see money as an object, and nothing more, you will become abundant in wealth because you will release yourself from the emotion of money. This may sound strange at first, but it will help to free you from any trace of a fear or greed mentality.

Think of wealth as a score that you are trying to achieve in an exam. The last time you sat the paper you got 80 out of 100. You might desire to reach 90 or 95 the next time you take the test because you want to be better. That is a good goal. The emotions that will drive you on to hit your target number (or score), however, are determination and achievement – not greed. Likewise, if you were aware that 70 out of 100 was a fail, you would be driven by the same motivations of wanting to make the grade – not the fear of losing money.

You cannot win without losing

Did you know that in the entire history of boxing there have only ever been a dozen or so world champions who have retired undefeated? And at the very pinnacle of the sport, in the heavyweight division, only the legendary Rocky Marciano has achieved that feat – defending his title six times between 1952 and 1956. In life, it is almost impossible to become a success without failing from time to time. In fact, any world champion in any sport will tell you that while they hate losing more than anything else, their defeats taught them more than their victories.

Like any business, the stock markets operate by supply and demand, and the long-term game is almost always the safest. Things do not always move in straight lines and often you have to hold your breath and get uncomfortable before you come up with a winning hand. As long as you are trading with capital that you do not depend upon for your lifestyle and well-being (i.e. you didn't borrow it, need it for bills, or steal it), you should be able to accept the occasional loss.

The reason that I talk about patience being important in trading (and I'd refer you to Warren Buffett's quote from earlier) is that generally speaking, when an event happens to make people start selling a stock, the price is going to drop. Like lemmings, more people will then panic (without doing any research) and sell. People are selling because they are fearful. Because this is a numbers game – and if you have done enough research, history will tell you this in the vast majority of cases – those stocks are highly likely to rise again at some point. It is a statistical fact. Now, before you run off and buy a falling stock and then come back and try to sue me when it doesn't recover, there are exceptions to the rule. But, generally speaking, patience and the ability to treat money that you can afford to lose as a number on a scorecard are all you need to win as a trader in the long term.

It is for this reason that, in my business, we employ a dedicated mindset coach, just to make sure no one brings emotional baggage or outside stresses and concerns onto the trading floor. If someone arrives for work here after the morning from hell – banged their toe getting out of bed, cut themselves shaving, stuck in traffic, tore their shirt on a door, etc. – we'd send them home. It's not that they're having an unlucky day, just that their mindset is all in the wrong place.

Here are two truths that you can rely upon: first, to make £1m as a trader you will have to lose £500k along the way. It will go something like this – you'll make £100k then drop to £80k, go up to £110k then back down to £90k, back up to £130k and so on. If you don't think you have the stomach (and mindset) for losing half a million pounds, go and find another way to make your first million. Second, the trader who tries to make money with a 100% track record will almost certainly blow their whole account first.

2. Education is crucial

My second big lesson is to encourage people to get smart. Too many people approach trading like they would a fruit machine or the roulette table – have a go and see how they get on. It simply does not work that way. You need to allocate time to get smart and understand the rules. Then you need to be constantly studying the news and the markets, learning about the companies that interest you, and watching the values of various stocks.

Believe me, there are a lot of talkers in this industry, and they will take your money in return for their fancy speeches as quickly as a casino would accept an all-in bet on red five. When you choose to learn how to trade or any skill in life, be smart and take advice from people who have been there and done that and proven that they know how to win.

We live in a world where it has never been easier to access information. Yes, there is a whole lot of fake news out there, and scammers are infiltrating everything trying to make money from the innocent – but the volume of good information still far outweighs the bad. In most cases, if you are diligent and stay well informed it is easy to spot the truth from the lies – you just need to do your research and refer to people that you do trust. Once you have found a safe and trusted source of education, learn as much as you possibly can.

Most people go through life thinking that it is OK for others because they are smart, or assuming that the person who just drove past them in a Ferarri was born rich. The truth is that most people are just lazy and frightened that investing in learning a new skill won't pay off. And here is the killer fact: if you step out from the majority and actually do something (because most people reading this won't), you suddenly put yourself in the 20% of people who might just own part of the 80% of wealth out there. How's that for a lesson in trading?

But, as I said, because learning new stuff is hard, being bold and trying something new is uncomfortable, the road looks too difficult, or you don't believe that you can be prosperous – most people won't act. They also base their idea of education on their previous experiences of learning at school. Well, I am certainly not an academic either. I got three Cs, a few Ds and mostly Fs in my GCSEs, but this year I am sitting my CISI (Chartered Institute for Securities & Investment) and IMC (Investment Management Certificate) exams. I don't need to do this since I already run a successful trading company, but I want to push myself into the unknown, knowing that it will benefit me next year.

3. Understand the broader picture of trading

In the trading world there are two camps. People think of themselves as either a fundamental or a technical trader. I simply do not understand the war of words, styles, and opinions between these two approaches. Why not just learn and apply both?

Technical analysis basically means looking at the stock chart and deciding the price of shares based on the technical data the chart is telling you. It assumes that price and volume are the only factors that will decide the likely movement of a stock and trends and patterns are used to predict what it might do in the future. It also takes into account support and resistance levels (which is people's predictable tendency to buy and sell on whole numbers – whereas the profit is often found to the right of the decimal point).

Fundamental analysis looks below the surface of the chart and interrogates the data to find out what is making it tick. Instead of simply looking at the numbers, you would be looking to understand the intrinsic value of the stock and attempting to predict the future value of the stock or currency. This means looking at the market as a whole, studying industry conditions, reading the news (including publications like 'non-farm payroll') and even looking into specific companies. You need to examine a company's earnings per share, profit to earnings ratio in the market, market cap, year on year profits, growth projections, and whether the brokers are rating the company as a buy, sell, or hold. In the Forex markets, you might need to look at the Consumer

Price and Retail Price indexes, the Bank of England interest rates, and so on. As I said in top tip number two – there is a lot to learn and study.

My point here, though, is not to get caught up in one camp or the other. There are two sides to every coin and seeing both very clearly will give you an advantage over those who are too single-minded. If you are prepared to put in the extra work that is.

4. Be patient

Another great quote from Warren Buffett goes like this: 'The stock market is a form of taking money from the impatient and giving it to the patient.'

I've already talked about this from an actual trading point of view and being patient while you are waiting for the right time to sell or buy a stock. But it is also an important aspect to apply in anything that you decide to pursue in your life. Yes, time is precious, and we all want to live our dreams now – but life does not work that way. You can enjoy your time now, while you are working towards your bigger goals, by all means; but trying to get there too quickly will hinder your progress. Patience isn't just a virtue; it paves the pathway to success.

Someone once said, 'it took me twenty years to become an overnight success', and I think that a version of this saying is true of almost every successful person in any walk of life.

In the same way that world champion boxers rarely remain undefeated throughout their entire careers, you simply cannot find success overnight. It takes hard work, dedication, good training, and the right mindset. I suppose that is why so many people who dream of prosperity simply put their faith in the longest odds of all – the lottery – because all they are prepared to do is dream.

Trading is not a get rich quick scheme – it is a way to achieve prosperity (in all its forms and definitions) through the application and understanding of the algorithms (or rules) of life and self-development.

Let me finish off this section about patience with the story of the Chinese bamboo.

Like most plants, the Chinese bamboo starts with a seed planted deep under the ground. Provided that it gets the right nurturing (water, good soil, and warmth), it will begin to grow in the depths of the earth, ready for the time when it breaks the surface and shows itself to the world.

Unlike most other plants, however, the Chinese bamboo is patiently preparing itself for one of the most remarkable feats of growth on the entire planet. After year one, there are no visible signs of growth; likewise, year two passes without a peak. By years three and four the uninformed (or impatient) observer would probably have given up hope and sought out another, more reliable, bamboo. But then, in its fifth year, the Chinese bamboo proves that patience and preparation can truly deliver.

As that first shoot finds the sunlight, all that pent-up energy bursts forth and the bamboo begins to grow. And boy, does it grow! Stretching towards the sky, at a rate of 2 feet per day (yes, per day), the Chinese bamboo becomes a 90-foot giant within just a month and a half, after spending five whole years lying seemingly dormant in the ground.

How's that for a long-term investment?

So, there are some of the biggest lessons I've learned from my first ten years as a trader. Now, let me share with you some of the stories about how I learned them.

'Bad stuff just happens – you get to choose what happens next.'

Chapter 2

SCHOOL WAS AN EDUCATION

School was a real education for me, but not in the academic sense of the word. It was brutal – and it changed me into the worst version of myself. A person who I barely recognise today, but one who had great qualities hidden below the surface just waiting for an opportunity to break out.

This idea of having different 'versions' of who we are is an important thing to understand before we move on because we are all ourselves to the core. It is just that our circumstances (both the ones we choose and the ones fate chooses for us) and the decisions we make determine which version of us goes on to control our lives. Too many people just drift and let life, luck, and laziness shape their path. Some even allow themselves to dream, work hard, and put up a fight – from time to time – but ultimately settle for being ordinary. But if just one person, after reading this book, decides to escape one of the generalised stereotypes I've just described, my mission is accomplished. Although I sincerely hope it will be hundreds or tens of thousands of people (including you).

You see, everything in life is a choice. You cannot always determine what happens, but you always get to choose how you react to what happens. When life throws obstacles in your way, you get to choose whether you walk the worn path with the crowd, or cut your own path and see what lies on the other side.

Then, when you've seen the place that you want to go, you just need to keep going until you get there. And I'm not just talking about blind determination; I'm talking about learning the route, making a plan, and pursuing it with everything that you've got.

A beacon of decency

My first school was called Knutsford Primary School, in Watford. The headmaster, Mr Nicholson, was someone I really looked up to and, even to this day, his seemingly superhuman ability to remember every single person's name is a skill I aspire to emulate. My lasting impression of my time at Knutsford, however, was the day the entire school burnt down – and I mean completely. It was Monday, 1 November 1999, and it was a teachers' inset day, so we were not due in school anyway. You could see the smoke for miles, and it wasn't long before the rumour mill (by phone, of course, because Twitter hadn't been invented by then) began circulating the story.

Looking back, it was a shocking thing to have happened, and we were all very fortunate that it had begun early in the morning before anyone was on site. The final verdict was that it was an accidental fire started by an electrical fault, but that didn't stop us speculating. Apart from the immediate benefits of our extra one-day holiday being extended to an entire week, the wild imagining sparked off in our minds by such an eerie event was exhilarating. What I didn't realise, at the time, is that what happened after the fire would have more of a lasting impact on my life than the destructive blaze itself.

I still remember Mr Nicholson being interviewed on TV, and being quietly impressed with how calm and measured he was. That was my headteacher – who knew my name and always smiled and said, 'hello Samuel' when he saw me – speaking on the news. Being on TV was an even bigger deal back then, as cable was still in its infancy and pretty much everyone I knew still only had access to the four terrestrial channels.

By the end of that week, Mr Nicholson had reopened the school, and we spent the next few years in pop-up classrooms made of portacabins. But he remained unflappable and professional throughout the whole process. As I said, I didn't realise it at the time (and I'd like to think he will get to read these words one day), but I believe that his constant integrity and resilience somehow lodged somewhere within my own character during that period of my life.

Out of the fire and into the firing line

From Knutsford, I followed James (my older brother) to Bushey Hall School which, at the time, had something of a reputation. The fact that it consistently performed below the government exam result targets over 20 years, and had been in the OFSTED failure category twice, is just touching the surface. Perhaps if I tell you that, at times, we had a full-time police presence on site, it might give you more of a clue of what it was like to spend five years going there.

This was a case of being taken out of the fire and thrown in front of the firing line. As I said at the start of this chapter: it was brutal. And if Mr Nicholson had instilled any kind of ethics and honesty in that young and highly impressionable version of me, Bushey Hall was about to beat it back out.

In a rough environment, you need to learn quickly and adapt or you simply won't last. One of the skills I picked up in my first few weeks at Bushey Hall was how to look out for fireworks flying down the cloisters. I'm serious, it was a regular occurrence and, as far as I could tell, no one even tried to do anything to stop it. Many years later, when I watched *The Hunger Games* for the first time, it very nearly gave me flashbacks. It wasn't just rockets that lit up the imagination of the school's pyromaniacs either – it was also advisable to check your backpack before putting it on because they would attach Catherine wheels (we called them 'spinning Marys') to unsuspecting kids' bags and light them as they walked past.

On one occasion, again innocently walking down the cloisters, someone ran a Stanley knife across my back, through my blazer and shirt, and into my skin – leaving a scar which I still bear to this day. I don't know who did it, I never found out why, and maybe it was no more than a dare. But it was another one of those pivotal moments in my passage towards the darker version of me.

As I saw it, I had two choices at this point: stop going to school or join them. I tried both and, while nobody seemed to care if I didn't turn up for days on end, I eventually set off along the latter path. It was not an easy transition, and it brought more scars and playground battles, but at least I was one of the crowd and a less obvious target. This new-found position among the troublemakers didn't keep me free from pain though, and during one particularly boring English lesson I got into an argument with another boy who subsequently stabbed me through the hand with a fountain pen. Again, I still have the scar today, but it was the look on the teacher's face, just before she fainted, that will be my lasting memory of that experience.

It was around this time that I started boxing. I'd been into martial arts since I was at junior school, mostly as a form of physical exercise, but boxing felt more like answering the call of the violence inside of me. I was angry and, particularly during those last few years of school, there had to be a way of getting that anger out. Boxing fit the bill perfectly, though it also sparked off another trait in me that I would later come to recognise as an asset and that has served me well ever since. But at that time, it was purely the anger that I felt each time I went to the gym or stepped into a ring to spar. Boxing became a way of surviving: both physically and emotionally. (I'll pick up on this part of the story in the next chapter.)

Expelled for conforming

I have learned that, in life, there are both reasons and excuses. You can blame the system, the environment, fate, or other people's cruelty as much as you like (those are the excuses), or you can deal with life. Bushey Hall School was not a learning environment, and no one came out of that place with great grades. The bullying and bad behaviour were out of control, no one could escape it, and I had no say in being there. It was deal with it, join in, or run away.

There were genuine reasons that I was going in a poor direction, but I can't make excuses for myself. Looking back, I have realised that bad stuff just happens – but you get to choose what happens next.

On top of that, things were getting bad at home, and the situation eventually led to my parents getting divorced. Having grown up in a loving family, where home meant sanctuary and the four walls of our house were a barricade from whatever was going on outside, divorce completely changed our family dynamic. I don't blame my parents (as I have grown up myself, I've seen how love and circumstance can be fickle partners), but it did add an extra level of pressure at a turbulent time in my life. So, I moved from a lovely home in Bricket Wood to a one-bedroom, half-way-house flat in Percy Road, Watford. There I lived with my Dad and my brother; and we had the company of the down, the out, and the desperate for neighbours. It was a dark time with few opportunities for any light to find its way through.

Looking back now I can see that, at my core, I was still me; it was a version where all the good was restricted and the darkness was free to flourish, but it was definitely me. I'm not justifying or glorifying what I became by any means, but there were some strong characteristics on display for sure. I was outwardly confident and fearless, I'd learned how to watch my back, my resilience levels were through the roof, and I quickly learned who I could trust and who was worse than me.

I had spiralled into the darkness of my environment and allowed it to influence the quiet, impressionable kid who had innocently walked through its doors some four years earlier. Having experienced the influence of a good role model, I was perhaps looking for more and found that my aspirations were disappointed. This led to several confrontations with the authorities, being expelled, and only getting two GCSEs to show for my rebellion.

James – my older brother – had left four years earlier, joined the police in 2009, and eventually the Counter-Terrorism Armed Response Unit. (His Bushey Hall experience had clearly had a different effect on him.) I left without a clue what I would do next and started to spend a lot of time on my Xbox.

For the record, Bushey Hall School transformed into Bushey Hall Academy in 2009 and, from what I understand, has become a true bastion of outstanding Hertfordshire education for young people living in Watford.

'I wanted to be the best that I could be, so I started to study the best in the world.'

Chapter 3

BOXING CLEVER

Boxing is the oldest, simplest, and perhaps most noble sport in the world. Throughout the ages, it has evolved, become regulated, increased in skill, and lessened in mortality, but it is still essentially the same face-to-face combat that it was many thousands of years ago. Modern boxing, at its highest professional level, with all its razzmatazz, glittering lights, build-up, boastings, and pay-per-view, is something of a spectacle to behold. But at its core, just as it always was, it is two people facing each other with nothing but fists, strength, courage, speed, and skill between them. As someone once said, 'you play football, you play rugby, but you don't play boxing'.

But it is fair to say that boxing is not everyone's cup of tea.

There are three types of reaction to anything that you are presented with in life. You love it, you hate it, or you are completely indifferent. The most common of these traits is indifference: you can take or leave romantic comedies; vegetables are something you eat because they are there; you excuse your friends' poor attitudes as 'just the way they are'; and you need to have 'a' job to pay the bills. The problem with indifference is that it is weak. No one, ever, in the entire history of humanity, changed their life circumstances or achieved anything of any significance through indifference.

To be motivated to change something, you must either love it or hate it. Nothing will ever change in your life, nor will you be able to meaningfully change the lives of those who you love, until the love of your vision or the hatred of your circumstance overwhelm you and compel you to act. And you must also, of course, believe that you are able.

The reason that boxing is such a great analogy for achievement in life is that you cannot succeed in it, or in truth even start to compete, until you are committed to the course. You must love the fight, hate your opponent (at least temporarily), and believe deep down to your core that you can win. It is not a sport that you can enter into indifferently – to do so would mean pain, defeat, and demoralisation.

Even if you are someone who dislikes (or even hates) boxing (and if that is you, thank you for reading this far into the chapter and please bear with me), I hope that you see my point. Most people in life are indifferent about achieving greatness. They either don't believe in themselves enough, or they don't feel passionately enough about changing their circumstances. The fact is that 'you' need to change 'you' first – and that takes guts, determination, belief, bravery, and either love or hate as fuel. Whatever you think about boxing, as a sport, you need to take a boxer's attitude in life if you want to achieve anything more than being ordinary.

But here is the big lesson to take away from boxing: there is so much more to it than brutally and angrily swinging your fists at an opponent. It is the ultimate test of skill, analytics, awareness, reaction, and strength (both mental and physical). And that is what we are going to discover in this chapter.

The ancient art of the old one-two

I started martial arts lessons, on and off, from the age of 11; but in both disciplines that I tried (Aikido and Jiu-Jitsu) I eventually gave up because I didn't like being told off by the instructors. I think the description 'discipline' was quite apt at the time. Growing up, I was always essentially an all-or-nothing kind of person, and I either excelled or quit – there was no middle ground.

Some of my more successful (if not somewhat unconventional) pursuits included: roller hockey, where my team finished in the top ten in the UK; trampolining for the Ministry of Air competition team; and I even came close to representing the Great Britain international tenpin bowling team. If I was passionate about something, I would give it my all. And if I failed or came second (as was often the case), I would torment myself for weeks trying to work out where I failed or what I could have done better.

My involvement in boxing stemmed from self-preservation and anger. It was towards the end of my time at Bushey Hall school, and I felt vulnerable and on the defensive pretty much every day. Boxing seemed like an ideal way to channel my growing anger and aggression, while also having the benefit of making me 'pretty useful' if I got into a fight. I figured that if word got around that I was a boxer, people might leave me alone – and, eventually, it worked.

I loved boxing from the very first day I walked into my local club. I loved the feeling of being strong, the excitement of anticipating my opponent's next move, the buzz of being surrounded by adrenaline, and even the thrill of taking a punch. But the thing I loved most of all was recognising patterns, analysing behaviours, and adapting other people's styles into my own. And I don't just mean the actions of my trainers and the people I trained alongside. I wanted to be the best that I could be, so I started to study the best in the world – past and present. I also discovered that inside this ancient art of one-on-one, hand-to-hand combat was hidden a treasure trove of life skills. It was so much more than the old-fashioned one-two and then jab, or the famous uppercut or mighty knock-out punch. It was a game of wisdom, skill, speed, and most of all heart. Here are some of the things I learned from the best in the world.

Jack Dempsey

I discovered this guy called Jack Dempsey (Heavy-weight Champion of the World from 1919 to 1926) watching black and white footage on YouTube, and his story fascinated me. He was born into a poor family and faced a rough, tough childhood growing up on the streets in Manassa, Colorado, with little or no prospects in life. Perhaps, at first telling, you would think that is a stereotypical boxer's story and that they all start that way – but consider how many other kids whose lives start like that never break free. Those that do truly earn it. Jack Dempsey had heart and was driven by a need to survive. His survival ultimately took him to the top of the world, but there were (and still are) many millions of people just like him who chose not to survive.

> *'When I was a young fellow, I was knocked down plenty. I wanted to stay down, but I couldn't. I had to collect the two dollars for winning or go hungry. I had to get up. I was one of those hungry fighters. You could have hit me on the chin with a sledgehammer for five dollars. When you haven't eaten for two days, you'll understand.'*
>
> Jack Dempsey

Dempsey became known as 'The Manassa Mauler' on account of his ferocious and aggressive style and phenomenal punching power. In his day, the rules were that you fought until you finished and that often meant the loser (and occasionally the winner too) were unrecognisable after the fight – even to their nearest and dearest. I dare you to go and look him up now and see how brutal his world was, and then you might understand why they used to have whiskey in the corner between rounds instead of water.

My big lesson from Jack Dempsey is that you should never stay down. Because if you are feeling the pressure and are ready to throw in the towel, it is likely that your opponent is too – and you only need to keep going longer than them to win. I used this in the ring and have translated it into life circumstances too – and it works. You will be amazed at how many times your competition gives in just after you have said to yourself 'come on – give it one more round'.

And even if you do sometimes lose (it happens to the best of us), make sure you learn from the experience, shake yourself down, and have another go. Another of my favourite quotes from Dempsey after losing a fight was: 'Tell him he can have my title, but I want it back in the morning.'

Mike Tyson

Known as 'the baddest man on the planet' during his fighting years, and to the untrained eye a brute of a fighter, it was actually Mike Tyson who showed me that the history of the sport mattered. Watching him in an interview one day, he talked in great depth about the hours he spent learning about other fighters, watching what they did, and applying what he learned to his own style. He was so much more than the fierce fighting machine that you saw once he entered the ring. Mike Tyson was a thinker and an intelligent man who knew that opponents who feared him were weaker for it – so he invested in building that fear and becoming known for being bad.

On a practical level, Mike Tyson was the master of the body shot, and that meant he focused a lot of his time in the gym on pad work. He was famous for it, and his pad routines were amazing. So, I simply stole them and made them my own. After all, he had stolen them from the people he idolised in the first place.

> '*I'm the best ever. There's never been anybody as ruthless. I'm Sonny Liston, I'm Jack Dempsey. There's no one like me. I'm from their cloth.*'
>
> Mike Tyson

My biggest lesson from Mike Tyson is that you don't need to work everything out for yourself. There have been generations of successful people passing on the things that they learned from the change-makers that went before them. And all we need to do is listen, observe, understand, and apply what made them great to the uniqueness that exists inside each one of us. It is that simple.

Muhammad Ali

Imagine describing someone using just one simple, generic word, without any reference to sport, politics, science, the arts, or even a particular nation or era, and everyone knows who you are referring to. Muhammad Ali was undisputedly the 'greatest'. Yes, it was an audacious self-proclamation, but he backed up his words and, even though he suffered several humiliating defeats during his career, no one doubted him in the end.

> *'Only a man who knows what it is like to be defeated can reach down to the bottom of his soul and come up with the extra ounce of power it takes to win when the match is even.'*
>
> Muhammad Ali

Ali was known for his speed and his jab. He was like lightning around the ring, always moving, always dancing, always ready to close in with a volley of jabs and then quickly escape anything coming back the other way. In his day he was absolutely unbeatable. But what really made the great man the champion that every other sportsperson looks to as their inspiration was that he understood his environment. He was a champion in the ring, but what made him the 'greatest' was that he also controlled what happened outside of the ring.

A great example of this was the build-up to the famous 'Rumble in the Jungle', in 1974, between him and his long-time rival George Foreman, the then undefeated heavyweight champion of the world. Held in Zaire (now the Democratic Republic of the Congo), the fight was watched by 60 000 fans in the huge open-air stadium, and over one billion on TV around the world, smashing the viewing figure records for that time. It was a tense affair in the build-up and Ali's usual banter and razor-sharp rhymes added to the edge and rivalry that brewed before the two warriors entered the ring.

The whole event deserves a book in itself, but one of the things that stood out to me was how Ali won over the people of Zaire and compelled them to adopt him as their hometown fighter. His relaxed style, mixing with the people and speaking to them in the street, contrasted massively with Foreman, who touched down with all the glitz and glamour in his private jet accompanied by his German Shepherd dog. Foreman clearly didn't know (or maybe didn't care) that historically, while under Belgian occupation, the breed had been used by the police to control the people of that nation. The predominately black population interpreted this as a symbol of white oppression, and Ali was fully prepared to capitalise on Foreman's error (he would have made a great trader). He became the people's hero and won their hearts long before he won the fight. There is no doubt in my mind that the great man had planned this well in advance (knowing that Foreman took his dog everywhere) because he understood that home support would play a crucial part in the build-up to the rumble.

My biggest lesson from Muhammad Ali is simply to be prepared and don't leave anything to chance. When it comes to trading, for example, the more you know about a specific company, the marketplace in general, any extenuating circumstances, the news, the controlling board, the customers of that business, historical performance, and any issue or detail that you can discover, the more likely you are to make a decision that will reward your investment.

Joe Frazier

If Mike Tyson created a pre-fight impression of intimidation, then surely 'Smokin' Joe Frazier's relentless fighting style was even more irresistible as the first bell rang. From the moment the fight started, he would just keep moving forward, swinging his arms and never letting up, giving his opponent very little room to rest, breathe or recover.

Frazier reigned as undisputed Champion of the world from 1970 to 1973 and was involved in many of the great fights in boxing history, including legendary bouts with Muhammad Ali and George Foreman. Like all great fighters he was likened to those who had gone before him, and in Smokin' Joe's case these were Henry Armstrong and Rocky Marciano. But I think this sort of comparison, while representing a great compliment to the subject, has the potential to overshadow the truth of the matter. And in doing so, it hides one of the biggest secrets to success.

You see, it is not an accident that fighters (or any sportspeople for that matter) resemble superstars from bygone eras. Because it is not resemblance at all, it is imitation and inspiration that is at work. Whether knowingly or not, any student of a subject will be influenced to copy or build upon those whose work they admire. This is true in the music industry, throughout the history of art, across political systems and ideologies, at the core of all religions, and, most importantly (for the purposes of this book at least), in the lives of the commercially successful and mega-wealthy.

When I was studying my boxing heroes, in between pushing my body to the limit at the gym, I was massively attracted to the style of Joe Frazier. He just kept coming forward. Whatever defence his opponent threw at him, however determined to stand their ground they were, he just kept walking forward, swinging overhand blows as he advanced.

He was relentless and – combined with his strength, resilience, and famous left hook – it made him a very hard man to beat. And he could only fight like that because he worked harder than anyone else in the gym when no one else was looking.

'You can map out a fight plan or a life plan, but when the action starts, it may not go the way you planned, and you're down to your reflexes – that means your [preparation]. That's where your roadwork shows. If you cheated on that in the dark of the morning, well, you're going to get found out now, under the bright lights.'

Joe Frazier

So, whenever I got in the ring, I just stepped into the Joe Frazier part of the boxing persona I had created for myself and I determined in my heart and mind that I was going to keep walking forward. I am like this in business and in the other important areas of my life too – if something has value for me, I will just keep moving towards it until I get there. And I owe much of this attitude to Smokin' Joe Frazier.

My biggest lesson from Joe Frazier is never to stop advancing. The ability to react to circumstances is critical if you want to be successful in boxing or business. But it is far better to be in control of the pace, the momentum, and the direction of a project or a fight.

George Foreman

I've left George Foreman till last, for two reasons. First, because his training routines were so intelligent and focused on a particular purpose; and second, because he discovered a simple way to turn his name into a healthy profit after he had finished boxing.

His legacy includes being the two-time Heavyweight Champion of the World and having an incredibly long career for a heavyweight boxer. After winning the Olympic gold medal in 1968, he fought his final professional fight in 1997 aged 48. He did have a 10-year break in the middle of that period, but in my book that makes his achievement even more impressive.

Foreman was known for his outrageously strong big-hitting style in the ring, and his bag work (using the punch-bag, during a training session) in the gym. He even created his own training routines to help him prepare for specific fights and fighters. You could even liken these to a type of algorithm that he employed to increase his efficiency. As an obsessive student of boxing, I was always able to recognise these patterns and would often open conversations in the gym with comments like: 'I see you are a fan of Foreman's bag work then.'

One particular routine that he designed was purely as a defence against Muhammad Ali's jab. He would hit the bag 10 times on one side, then once with his heavy hand (his strongest punching arm) on the other side. Then he would repeat the 10 on the first side, followed by 2 on his strongest, then 10 and 3, 10 and 4, and so on. He was determined that his hands would not drop during the fight and leave him exposed to Ali's jab, and so he just kept on training until he was ready. I used this a lot in my own routines and loved being able to learn from another of my heroes.

George always gave the credit for his longevity and great physique to his healthy eating style, and it was this that attracted Salton Inc. to ask for his endorsement and name on their fat-reducing grill. It is estimated that he has earned over $200 million from sales of 'The George Foreman Lean Mean Fat-Reducing Grilling Machine', simply by turning up for a few days' filming and photo shoots. If that is not monetisation of an asset (in his case his name and reputation), then I do not know what is. Foreman simply identified, like many other famous sportspeople and celebrities do, that their brand has value.

> *'Money is a good thing, but every morning you have to get up with something no one else in the world gets up with – that's that image. That face you see in the mirror, you got to love it, and you better do some things that you feel good about inside of you. Of course, money is going to come, but make certain that you do some good with it.'*
>
> George Foreman

My biggest lesson from George Foreman was copying his bag work routines when I was training as a boxer myself and understanding the value of a strong brand as I learned to trade. In very simple terms, bad news and uncertainty often cause the share prices of well-known companies to drop quickly and significantly. Having done your research into that business (caveat: this is not 100% guaranteed strategy) – and identifying that its reputation, culture, resilience, and structure is sound – I would expect that brand to revive over the short or long term. If people believe in a brand, and smart people recognise that belief, it will always make money.

Box clever and learn

There are, of course, many other boxers who have graced the ring and left their unique and indelible mark upon the canvas. But the ones I've shared with you here are some of my favourites.

You will notice that I have added quotes from each of the boxers I've profiled here, and perhaps it is more traditional for inspirational one-liners to be uttered by world-changing leaders, influential orators, or poets. But you don't need to look far to find enormous wisdom from the heart and minds of great boxers because these people are not brutes – they are thinkers, analysers, and risk managers who know how to channel their love and hate into however many 3-minute rounds it takes to get the job done.

I officially retired from my amateur boxing career five years ago, and one of the biggest impacts that it had on me was that when I started, I was intensely angry – and by the time I'd finished, I wasn't angry anymore.

'All I needed to add was my energy, self-belief, and 100% commitment.'

Chapter 4

TRADING FATE FOR FORTUNE

Despite my Bushey Hall experience, something inside me still made me think that there would be value in getting an education. So, I applied for college and happily set off for the entry interview without even considering that I might not meet the requirements. Everything went well and when they asked if I had the achieved the required GCSE exam results I simply said 'yes' and promised to bring them in another time.

The college required a minimum of five GCSE passes (level C or higher). I had just two and, in all honesty, I think I was lucky to have been awarded them. Clearly, there were a few rules to be broken here, so I called on the services of Photoshop to replace five years of mis-spent schooling with two hours of meticulous design work. As far as I was concerned I had nothing to lose and, although I still feel I little bit guilty to this day, it did teach me another big lesson: most people are far too lazy to double-check anything.

So, in September 2007, I started an IT and Networking course at college. My first day was great, meeting new people and feeling like I might actually learn something, then it all went downhill from there. My education mindset had become 'turn up when you want to' and 'sleep in' when you don't, so I just let this continue. The only difference with the college's approach to discipline was that they didn't chase me up or check where I was – it seemed they expected me to take responsibility for my own behaviour. Well,

I was nowhere near that level of maturity, so I was quite surprised when, after a couple of months, I turned up late one morning only to be thrown off the course.

I still remember the resigned look on my Dad's face when I came home and told him the news, before disappearing into my room to play Call of Duty for the next 12 months. (I learned so much more than you will believe during that time, but I'll share some Black Ops wisdom with you in the next chapter). Years later, my Dad explained that he had just got to the point with me where he felt the best thing was to let me get 'whatever it was' out of my system.

But even I never thought it would take me a whole year of virtual reality war games to get there.

Taking my second chance

After my year of Xbox exploits was up, and I realised that it would never become my career (even though I came close to landing a £30k a year job from it), I decided to go back to college. I'm not sure who laughed louder at the idea: my Dad or the same teacher who had previously dismissed me as a 'no show' when I called to ask if I could discuss it with him.

But, to give this teacher his due, he humoured me and agreed to talk it through. The meeting didn't start well as he was keen to explain how his performance was judged on a points system, based on how many students passed or completed each course. I was firmly in the category of having cost him a bucketload of points and, quite frankly, making him look incompetent. He was in no mood for charity and had clearly just agreed to the meeting so he could vent some frustration. But then something happened. From somewhere within me, I just decided that I could not fail again. I had failed this man sitting in front of me once – this man who had decided to devote his life to educating young people and giving them a chance to make something of themselves; I had failed me; and I had failed my parents' faith in me. So, I made him a promise – and it was a promise that I believed from deep down within my heart that I would keep. It was the sort of promise that I would have made to Mr Nicholson, had he been sitting in front of me that day. I promised that teacher that I would succeed.

I told him that I would never be late, I would always be at the top of his class, and I would make him proud to have taught me – this time I would earn him points. And I will forever be grateful that he believed me and gave me my second chance. Thank you, Kurt.

That year, everything changed for me. I worked hard, I studied outside of school, I stayed late, I arrived early, and I even learned how to be humble. On the one hand, I was thoroughly enjoying the feeling of being a success, but the other side of that shiny coin was the demoralising experience of seeing the people from my previous year progress on to their second and final year. Obviously, it wasn't quite a Bushey Hall level of being left outside of the cool gang, but it hurt all the same. And pretty much every day I had to deal with the knowledge that I was an entire year behind everyone else because of the decisions that I – and I alone – had made. If anything, however, this now had the effect of making me try even harder.

Another motivation to keep my word and succeed was when I learned that the top performer in each year would get a £2k bursary if they then went on to attend their local university. At that time, I didn't even know what a bursary was, but I liked the idea of having £2k to spend.

At the end of the year, I passed the course with three distinctions and finished where I promised – at the top of the class. What's more, I also achieved higher marks than any of the people in the previous year. I had achieved what I set out to do, and it felt great.

Attracted to wealth and enlightened by a liar

With my IT qualification under my belt, accompanied by an overwhelming feeling of being a success and the promise of £2k to go and study some more, the idea of earning real money also caught my attention. So, while my fellow college leavers were clear about the career path they would be pursuing, or the universities they would be applying to attend, my mind was torn. The £2k was appealing, but so was the idea of a well-paid job and a supercar.

Google told me that oil rig workers earned the most money, so I did some research and started to apply for positions drilling out on the open sea. I desperately tried to translate my limited experiences into transferable skills that might appeal, and I must have sent off dozens of application forms. Most of the roles asked for two, three, or five years' experience as a basic requirement, but I just figured that unless I started somewhere, I would not even set foot on the experience ladder. So, I just sent off application after application – with no reply. It seemed that, despite the attraction of £200k per year, the oil industry and I were never going to get along. Little did I know then that after gathering a handful of years' experience as a trader, I would soon be putting a few oil companies in their place. (I'll come back to that story in Chapter 10 a bit later).

During my search for the highest paid jobs going, I was also attracted to the banking sector. But my applications there met with the same silent response and my lack of experience wasn't opening any doors. While researching this area, however, I came across a seminar claiming to teach you how to trade the stock market and promising big returns. By now, I was determined to learn how to unlock this world of creating wealth, so I went off to hear what they had to say (persuading my slightly apprehensive Dad to come with me).

It was an enormous eye-opening revelation, and I could clearly see that there was an opportunity there somewhere. The only problem was that the people running that particular seminar were out to make money from suckers, not turn them into traders. Looking back, I am almost embarrassed to tell you just how far I got taken for a ride that day. But I made you a promise at the beginning of this book, to be honest and tell you everything, so here goes. The main speaker started by boasting how he had just flown back from a salmon fishing trip in Scotland, in his helicopter, just to run the seminar. As he talked about his life, career, and the trading secrets he had to share, pictures of his fast cars, big houses, exclusive family holidays in far-flung places, and exorbitant wealth flashed across the screen above him. The only bit of credit I'll give that man is that he sold well – and he sold me big time.

To get a piece of the action and find out all that he knew normally cost £3.5k, but as a special offer we could secure our future for just £2k – for one night only. Yes, I know, 'If it sounds too good to be true, it probably is!'

Wise, wary, and sensing-a-scam Dad said, 'I don't know about this Sam, I really don't think it is a good idea'. But enthusiastic, naive, and hungry-for-success Sam begged for the chance to change our lives forever. It turned out that Dad was right in the end – but maybe if he hadn't lent me pretty much everything he had that evening, I wouldn't have gone on to learn how to trade myself. Who knows? But he did get his dream boat out of it eventually. I must point out at this point that while Dad supplied the credit card on the night, he later petitioned my Mum to cover half the cost and, between them, they also bought me a laptop so I could start trading.

That course taught me one thing, and one thing only – that everything I needed to learn about trading was readily available on the internet. All I needed to add was my energy, self-belief, and 100% commitment. Generating the motivation for that was easy – I felt like I owed my parents big time, and nothing was going to stop me from paying them back.

Buying stock with my bursary

In 1993, a paper called 'The Role of Deliberate Practice in the Acquisition of Expert Performance' was written by Anders Ericsson, a professor at the University of Colorado. In it, he presents a concept suggesting that doing anything for 10 000 hours will make you an expert – practice makes perfect. I was unaware of this study at the time, but I soon found myself proving it in practice.

I finished college in May that year and, after my failed attempt at landing a high-paid job, I started at the University of Hertfordshire in September. After realising that there was an opportunity in trading, but also grasping the fact that I needed to learn how to do it for myself, I set about doing just that: I began to study. And I studied every hour I could find. I had a few months of uninterrupted study time before starting university, and then found a way to combine the two. As Arnold Schwarzenegger once said, if you are tired and you haven't got enough time – sleep faster.

During my first year at university, I would be working 100–120 hours per week, spread between my academic studies and my quest for trading mastery. I devoured everything that the internet had to tell me about trading; I read books about, and by, traders, I downloaded and consumed literally thousands of PDF documents explaining the markets (some of them I even translated from Chinese first), and I began to trade.

Mum and Dad had already given me more than they could afford, so my bursary money became my down payment on a future that I could only start to imagine back then sitting in my university campus digs. I didn't just invest wildly – everything was considered and measured. It was so important to me that I got this right, and the fact that the risk was always on my side meant I became obsessed with knowing everything about each business I was researching. In fact, sometimes I got so involved in the stories behind the companies I was investing in that I even started using Tate & Lyle sugar in my tea and ordering Domino's pizza. Often, the cost was more than the return, but I was investing, and I have never believed in half measures.

By the end of that first year, while I was still at university studying for a degree in computing, I had turned my £2k bursary money into £178k. And it had cost me nothing more than time, commitment, and self-belief.

What are you doing with your time today?

Now might be a good time to meet my best friend and discover how he also traded fate for fortune.

Meet Elliot Guinn

Back in the mid-1990s, my family moved to Bricket Wood, a small village in Hertfordshire. I was 5 years old at the time, and one afternoon, while retrieving my football from a neighbour's garden, I met Samuel and we became great friends. Although he was a year younger than me, he had an influence on me from an early age and I (almost always) ended up better off for it (occasionally we got ourselves into a whole heap of trouble).

We went to different schools, mine was in St Albans and Samuel's in Watford, but we would always hang out in the evenings and weekends. Alongside the usual sports, games, biking adventures, and general boyish mischief, we were also quite good at making a few quid. Samuel just had this entrepreneurial streak that meant he could spot an opportunity to get paid. And, as long as it was something he wanted to do – and he could see that the reward was worth the effort – he would have us working really hard. There were all sorts of odd job schemes and selling stuff we'd made to people down our street, but our main enterprise was car washing. We seriously cornered the car-washing market in Bricket Wood for many years – no one else stood a chance. We even had some customers on regular contracts where we would turn up, wash their car, and only then knock on the door to collect payment.

Growing up and taking life seriously

Unlike Samuel, I was quite suited to school (not that I was always totally innocent); and when not being drawn into his money-making schemes and extra-curricular endeavours, I studied hard and set my sights on a place a university. After completing my degree in Finance and Economics, I happily began walking the path that society (and destiny) had so nicely laid out for me by taking on a banking sector job in the city. While at university, I had already done a placement year at Lloyds as a Risk Analyst, so it was obvious to me that this was the right career to pursue.

Like almost everyone else who passed through middle-class schooling in St Albans, I was ready to settle into an ordinary future of a good job in the city, buying a house, working long hours, and living for the weekends. While at Lloyds, a few of my colleagues had got me interested in the stock market, and I made a little bit of money on the fall and rise of their price during the crash, but it was only a dabble.

Of course, all of this time I would still see Samuel in the evenings and at weekends, and we would talk about everything from Call of Duty to making money and hopes and dreams to boxing. I'd seen Samuel get into trading more seriously, and also recognised that he was doing well at it, so my interest had grown over time. But it wasn't until he set up Samuel & Co Trading that I started to realise just how big this could become.

Maybe my life pathway wasn't set in stone?

So, there I was; starting out on a great career with a giant of the global financial scene while helping my best mate run training events for trainee traders at the weekends. Everything was mapped out for me, and my future looked just perfect. I had good money coming in, a secure career path, and great prospects; my family were proud of my achievements and all the 'successful life' boxes were getting ticked. But I just couldn't help wondering: 'what if?'

So, in 2017, I joined Samuel & Co Trading, and reset the satnav of my ordinary career path. I am, by nature, very much more risk-averse than Samel; I realised that when I was a young age. I know that many people reading this will think that I was mad (some of my family certainly did), but I don't believe in gambling and I never will. I believe in taking measured risks where the odds are highly in my favour and where I believe in the determination, algorithm, and application that support that risk.

That is why I joined Samuel & Co Trading, and two years down the track it is delivering everything I had counted on it delivering – and more.

'Most people choose (by making no choice at all) to remain average.'

Chapter 5

MY CALL
TO DUTY

Ask any child which subjects they enjoy the most at school, and then ask their teacher which ones they excel at, and you'll get matching answers every single time. If global leaders or those in control of national curriculums and education planning were to pay attention to that single fact they could 'quite literally' change the world. I get the basic level of education idea – that every child should learn how to read, write, and do a little bit of maths. But what if, after that, they simply focused on the things that they really enjoyed doing? What if we created a whole generation of children who absolutely loved school and education because they were doing the things that they enjoyed?

I know some of you are already thinking that we would end up with nothing more than a load of brilliant film critics and music buffs, the world's best online gamers, and a handful of great football players and Olympic athletes. But bear with me, because there is more to this than initially meets the ear. There are children who genuinely enjoy maths and science; some are fascinated by the animal kingdom, biology, and what makes us work; others are keener to understand what goes on inside a PlayStation than to pick up a controller; and I've met 10-year-olds with incredible ambition and ideas about how to solve the world's problems. Yes, they may well be in the minority, but what percentage of the population end up becoming brain surgeons, rocket scientists, law-makers, archaeologists, and university professors anyway? In my experience, most children are hungry for knowledge – they just prefer to learn things that interest them.

Even if you've come with me this far into my please-everybody education rehash, you are probably now thinking that the majority of children will still only want to play games, browse the internet, or watch movies. Well, so what? I cannot think of a better way to learn anything than by fully immersing myself in the world of that subject – can you? I actually think that, given the opportunity to choose, a lot of children might even surprise us; and whatever they did choose, the second part of my revolution is where the real magic happens. It would mean a teacher's role becomes encouraging whatever the child enjoyed doing; then starting to identify the innate skills and interests that activity revealed in the individual. Before you know it, we would have schools full of enthusiastic young people focusing on skills that would actually make a difference in the world.

I realise this is just a high-level seed of an idea, and the details need further study, testing, and planning; I'd love to think that someone reading this book might even run with it one day. But the reality is that no one ever will, and that is because of the second big problem with the education system (and for most people the entire passage of their life). People are scared of doing things differently and accepting that there might just be another way – a better way – than what society has been doing for hundreds of years. If it ain't broken don't fix it – yes – but what if it is broken and no one seems to have noticed or acknowledged that it needs fixing? We need to change the way we think about education – and pretty much everything else …

The course taken by the majority is, by definition, average; and it is that which stops them becoming extraordinary.

Pursuing any passion unleashes ability

In the previous chapter, I mentioned the year that I spent playing on my Xbox after being kicked out of college. I know that my Dad was incredibly worried for me at the time and felt frustrated that he didn't really have any alternatives or advice to offer me. Whether out of intuition or desperation (I don't think either of us will ever know for sure), in the end he just left me to it. I suppose he was hoping that I would eventually get it out of my system. I have to own up that this was not part of some brilliant super-strategy to become a multi-millionaire over the next five years, but it certainly played a major part in the story that unfolded.

Now, I am not proposing that the route to life and business success, for every child, must include a year out aimlessly playing computer games. Nor do I want bored teenagers to go waving this book in their parents' faces as an argument for them getting more game-time. But I would like people to consider what is involved in playing most computer games (or indeed any play or entertainment-based pursuit). You see, to get good at anything, you must spend a lot of time doing that thing – as previously mentioned, some famous studies suggest that if you invest 10 000 hours into any skill, you will, by default, become an expert. The important thing here, however, is not just to do something – but to practise it, study it, proactively improve at it, and, most importantly of all, analyse your development.

In my business, we work with hundreds of would-be entrepreneurs and traders each year through our various training programmes. Some of the first questions we ask are to find out what they like doing and what they have been doing up to that point in their lives. This tells us a lot about the person and also opens the door to discovering some of the natural abilities that they might have and some of the skills that they have been (unknowingly) honing along the way. For example, a firefighter will have good, fast instincts and be practised in the ability to remove emotions from their decision-making under pressure. A primary school teacher will be well-versed in observing lots of avenues of activity (usually around 30–35) at the same time. Plumbers are usually able to see innovative solutions and workarounds, while still keeping within the all-important safety parameters of their profession. People who like sport often have a competitive edge to them and will not give up easily – football fans, in particular, seem able to remain fiercely loyal, even at the worst of times. Those who like to read or study history and science in their spare time have a remarkable aptitude for detail and remembering things. And mums are often blessed with hidden depths of love, patience, and resilience, beyond that of someone who hasn't known the experience of bringing a new life into the world.

None of these traits are a coincidence, nor are they little more than marginally based on the genes those people inherited. They are the result of a passion (nature) or a circumstance (nurture) sending them in a particular direction in life. Then, by choice or necessity, that activity takes up a large part of their life, they became good at it, and it gives them a range of skills.

Most people never stop to consider that they have skills, and even fewer ever decide to see if those skills could be used to improve their lives and the lives of those that they love. Most people choose (by making no choice at all) to remain average. I believe that everyone could be extraordinary and, by default, raise the universal bar of what is considered average.

Pursuing my call to duty

Call of Duty is a first-person shooter game available on most major gaming consoles; and from October 2008 to August 2009, I spent between 15 and 18 hours a day becoming the best in the world (almost). On the rare occasions that I had face-to-face interaction with people (often concerned family members) they would say things like, 'why are you wasting your time doing that?' or 'when are you going to go and do something useful with your life?' At the time, I didn't have any answers for them, but I knew one thing – I was doing what I wanted to do, and I was enjoying being me. Of course, there was a part of me worrying that they might be right and, as I said earlier, I couldn't honestly say that I saw this as part of a great master plan. But, looking back, I can see now that the enormous amount of time, emotion, and dedication that I put into Call of Duty was teaching and perfecting a whole range of seriously strong business and life skills.

There are many variations of the game, but the most popular is called Domination and is basically two teams trying to capture a flag. Each team is made up of six players who take on the role of the SAS, the

Marines, or one of the world's other famous Black Ops special forces units. Mostly, the players would be operating remotely (from the relative safety and comfort of their own bedrooms), communicating via headsets and a streaming internet connection. Once you have selected your team and challenged another one, you are ready to enter the grid and start fighting for honour, glory, and your life. And, just like real life, those who enter without a plan or a strategy are not likely to last long and are destined to fall short of even their most mediocre expectations.

To win at Call of Duty you had to work out your plan long before you entered the field of battle to start the business of capturing your opponents' flag. You needed a business plan.

I had around a dozen people to choose from in my squad, and I would pick the most appropriate six according to the opponents, the mission, and the specific battleground we were about to enter. For example, I would often pick a sniper to cover the back of our squad, looking out for enemy movement and warning of, or preferably nullifying, any potential threats. A few of the team had super-fast reactions and an eye for the tiniest pixel distortion that might just give away an enemy position. These guys would be at the front of any advance, steering our attack and executing the famous 'fingers to eyes, two sharp handshakes and a point in a particular direction' movement that you see in the movies. I was also lucky enough to have access to people who were natural defenders, all out attackers, or strategic thinkers who could come up with the most ludicrously clever ways to get the edge we needed.

One of these game-winning tactics that we perfected (and, as far as I know, no other team ever discovered) was throwing a frag (grenade) to within a five millimetre spot on a screen, over a roof, so that we could either stop an enemy or learn whether they were there or not. This was one of dozens of drills that we practised for hours on end, just so that we could win more games. It got to the level that every time we entered a battle, we all knew exactly what the other members of our team would be thinking, what they would do next, and how likely they would be to be able to pull off their role – often we didn't even need to communicate verbally at all.

We also knew most of the other better teams out there as well as we knew our own. We studied our opposition to the finest detail, learned their tactics, and knew exactly how they were going to perform. It was a kind of competitor analysis operation, and it made all the difference. If we were facing an attacking team, we made sure that we were ready for them and had our best defenders backing us up. If they were a more strategic squad, we would set about out-thinking them. No stone was left unturned, and that's how I almost landed myself a £30k salary from wasting my time for a year.

I died a thousand times

As a result of dedicating around 5000 hours of my life to a computer game, across a sunlight-starved 10-month period in 2008, I was awarded the second prize in the Call of Duty World Championships. It happens every year, and tens of thousands of people enter the competition – the prize being a salaried position working for the game developer. I was gutted to have only become the second best in the entire world, and the fact that someone else had out-manoeuvred my best game still bothers me to this day. But the skills that I learned that year have multiplied the salary I would have earned by at least 5000%, so perhaps I shouldn't grumble too much.

Call of Duty taught me how to create a team who could work together and get results that are far beyond the sum of its individual members' abilities. It taught me that strategy, planning, and vision are the keys to everything: those who had none (and that is the majority of people) were easily defeated, and I just needed to be better prepared than those who did. The game gave me confidence in my own voice, and I naturally found myself taking on the role of commander in most games simply because I could see the bigger picture. I learned to read situations and manage risks so that I was always in the most advantageous position before engaging my competition. And, most importantly of all, Call of Duty opened my eyes to the fact that the rules were actually just instructions to follow for ordinary players – and once you understood the rules completely, you could start to write your own.

The rules of computer games, like the rules of business and the rules of life, are just an algorithm. They are a set of opportunities, obstacles, certainties, probabilities, skills, and abilities all controlled and influenced by effort, energy, and cognitive inputs. In other words, life, like business, is just a game.

During my Call of Duty obsession, I must have died a thousand times. And each time, rather than looking at it as a defeat, I sat back and analysed every decision and every action to work out why. If it was a member of my team who had messed up, I still took that on as my responsibility and made sure I did my best to help them improve for next time. So, each time I played the game, I got better and moved further toward my target of becoming the best in the world. In my business, I have had failures too (in fact, allowing for failure is an important aspect of successful trading), but I have applied the same analytical approach to ensuring I never make the same mistake twice. Fortunately, no one has died as a result of my business errors, but that doesn't mean I take them any less seriously than if they had. You see, for it to be effective, it has to matter.

In life, I have had a few moments (some of which I have, and will, cover in this book) where I've had brushes with death or deep despair. I have fully come to terms with the fact that, as far as any of us really know, we only have one life to live. So, I have decided that I am going to play the best game that I possibly can. I will learn from my mistakes, learn from other people's mistakes, learn from every available resource I can find, spend time practising and perfecting my skills, not waste any time on activities with no benefit to my goals, and spend my time (the only truly limited resource on the planet) deliberately and extremely wisely.

I promised myself, on that day when Kurt accepted me back on my college course, that I would answer my true call to duty for the rest of my life.

'Anyone can change and make themselves into a better version of themselves.'

Chapter 6

TRUST TRAVELS

Becoming known around the world as a successful trader, running a business with over 60 staff, and setting up your own cryptocurrency can put you under intense pressure sometimes. I'm not suggesting for a moment that it is akin to lying awake at night trembling over how you are going to pay your family's heating bill in your one-bedroom flat, nor would I want to patronise those in situations like that by suggesting the comparison. But it can generate a similar kind of overwhelming, out-of-your-depth, fear. I know this to be true because when I talk to my Dad about some of the decisions and imaginings in my head, he can relate from the other side of the coin.

Understanding how to be responsible for my own well-being, and that of others, is one of the biggest lessons I had to learn as my story unfolded. At the end of the day, I have put myself in this position and it is down to me to deal with the consequences, good and bad. No one else is responsible for what I do each day – nor can I make them be. I say this because, whatever your situation in life as you read this book, the very same expectation should apply to you. Whether it is the pressures of success or struggle, you must take responsibility – and I also want you to know that you are completely able to do so. In fact, I promise you that you are.

The choices that you make, the actions that you take (these are two separate things by the way), and how you follow through on those self-made promises is your choice and no one else's. Circumstances may happen that are beyond your control, but you cannot blame anyone else for the way that you choose to act. That would be nothing more than making excuses. And there is one other thing that you must consider before you decide how you are going to react to your circumstances or pursue a whole new direction out of nothing more than your will and imagination. You need to realise that whatever you do (and that includes giving in or doing nothing) will have an effect on the people around you. Not maybe, and not hopefully no one will care or notice; your choices touch everyone around you. Your choices speak volumes about who you are. Your choices travel.

Actions speak louder than words

Picture your oldest, closest friend for a moment – the person who you love the most or perhaps trust the most. It might be your partner, perhaps a parent or sibling, or maybe just someone that you have known and shared experiences with for a very long time. Now imagine you've just witnessed a car crash together, they've happened across you crying at your desk, or you've just watched the latest blockbuster movie in each other's company. Now, tell me: could you predict 'exactly' what they would say next or how they would react in those situations? Of course, you could!

You see, people are predictable and will only ever do things out of character if there are seriously extenuating circumstances. And in those rare scenarios, chances are that they are acting in character anyway, it's just that the rules of the game have changed so much that all reasonable predictions go out of the window. We are often told things like you can tell a person's character within the first seven seconds of meeting them – and that you never get a second chance to make a first impression. Well, that is not quite true. Yes, you might form an opinion fairly quickly after meeting a new person, but that is not necessarily a lasting impression. There are many times in my life, and I'm sure in yours too, that I've taken an instant like or dislike to someone and on further acquaintance found that they were a completely different person. No matter how hard a person tries, the person who they truly are will not stay hidden for long.

My point here and the purpose of this chapter is to help you understand that other people will always judge you by the things that you do consistently. Whatever you think of yourself, and whatever other people think about you, your actions (over any given period of time) are an accurate description of who you are. If you always get up and fight on (like Jack Dempsey), then you are clearly a winner and will (provided you fight with clear purpose and direction) eventually reach your goals. If you give in and look for someone or something else to blame as soon as a problem comes against you, I would humbly suggest that you need to evaluate your mindset. (And that observation is without even knowing you).

People's actions leave clues as to who they truly are, and this is important for two reasons. First, you can take a good, hard, honest look at 'you' and the way you deal with life's circumstances and lay your strengths and weaknesses on the line before yourself. The good news is that if the person you see is stopping you from succeeding – you can change! And the rest of this book will show you how.

Second, you can start to evaluate the people around you (not for gossip's sake) and decide if they are people who are a good influence on your success or not. I'm not suggesting that you never speak to your perpetually despondent next-door neighbour again or that you take grumpy Uncle Charlie off your Christmas list – just that you are careful how much you let them influence your attitude.

Get into the habit of examining people's behaviours in pressure situations or when opportunities are presented to them. Include yourself in this experiment too, as objectively as you can, and start to evaluate which type of approach gets the better result: taking responsibility and acting; or complaining and looking for excuses. I can already tell you the answer – and

I expect that you'll have guessed it too – but I want you to go and try it for yourself.

What other people think does matter

I have just explained why observing other people's actions and attitudes is a good source of mindset education. But let me take you back to the beginning of this chapter, where I talked about my own reactions to pressure and success and how that affects the people around me. This matters a lot because I want to be one of those people who is a positive influence on everyone I meet. The more I have walked the paths of business success (and I hold my hands up to admit that I still have loads to learn – in fact, I'm excited by the prospect), the more the pressure to deal with what others think has grown.

As children, we were taught that 'sticks and stones could break our bones, but names would never hurt us'. There is an element of truth in this because you do need to become thick-skinned if you want to get through all the criticism and accusation that success will throw in your path. But you need to realise that sometimes what people say has some foundation. You also need to be honest enough to admit that criticism can hurt – especially when it is not true.

You might be thinking that you don't care what anyone else thinks about you – and sometimes I would agree that it doesn't really matter. But if you want to be successful in business, it matters a lot. (Don't get me wrong here, there have always been people in the world who amass great wealth through ill-gotten gains and rob innocent people to fund their own life of luxury. The fact is that the laws of decency and the warriors of justice don't always catch up with these rogues – some do manage to slip through the net forever). But if you want to be a genuine success – in human, financial, and life-affirming terms – then you need to manage your profile. And that starts with being honest with yourself about who you are, who you want to be, and what you want to achieve.

People will assume, if you are successful in business, that life is always rosy and you never have to deal with pressure. Likewise, they will assume that people who are struggling today will never be able to escape their circumstances. These assumptions and any that you, I, or anybody else make about a particular person are simply not true. Anyone can change and make themselves into a better version of themselves. It starts with self-assessment and self-honesty, then you start behaving in a way befitting of who you want to be, then others around will see (and won't be able to help but notice) the real you, and before you know it 'you' will be changing your situation.

You see, when you believe in you, others will begin to believe in you, and then that belief will become a reality. I'm not saying that positive thinking alone will change anyone's life. But the combination of belief (yours and those around you) and learning to adopt the common traits, behaviours, actions, and attitudes of successful people will (because those characteristics have been observable in winners for thousands of years). Do everything to the best of your ability, do everything as honestly as you possibly can, have faith in yourself, engender trust from others and build trust – because trust travels.

The young entrepreneur

I learned that trust travels when I was very young, even before I started school – I think that every child does. In those early, highly formative years, the home environment teaches you all about trust (positively or negatively) and starts to model the person that you will become. Of course, each person is genetically unique, and there will be elements of character, natural physique, and ability that you are born with – but the circumstances you are born into will start to shape you early on. As I've mentioned already in this chapter, and throughout the book, I still believe that regardless of nature and nurture every single person on the planet can still choose to better themselves and fight for their fortune or lie down and accept the hand fate has dealt them. I know this is true because of all the amazing people

I've studied over the years, my own experiences, and the lives of those who I've personally been involved in changing.

One of the first major things that every child unknowingly learns in life is trust. Depending on their environment and the circumstances they are born into they will quickly learn who they can depend on, who loves them (even before they know what love is), and who they feel safe around. It is why a crying child will often stop the moment they are placed in a parent's arms, or their face lights up when Mum or Dad smiles at them.

As life goes on and other people are introduced into young lives, they soon find that not everyone or everything in the world is as safe as home. Sadly, for some, even home can become an unsafe, untrustworthy haven.

For me and James, our early life at home, in the village of Bricket Wood, was a place full of love and happy memories; a place where trust blossomed. Looking back, I suspect that those days were also the birthplace of my entrepreneurial spirit. With both parents working, Mum came up with a scheme to get us helping with some of the chores around the house. She designed a kind of jobs board, with a range of tasks and rewards: from polishing the taps (20p) or putting out the rubbish (10p), to doing the washing up (30p) or hoovering the living room floor (50p). James would do his bit, but I saw this as an industry. Mum often reminds me of how she eventually had to limit the number of times I could do each task – which I think was a result of my first £30 month. I can still hear her exasperated plea, "the taps don't need polishing every day, Sam".

Together with my best friend, Elliot, we used to make pom-poms (probably something I'd seen on *Blue Peter*) and walk around the village knocking on doors to try and sell them to our neighbours as cat toys. Then, when we had sold out of pom-poms, we would go back down the same streets offering to wash cars or take on any other odd jobs that people needed doing. Maybe it was the nature of the village community, or perhaps the fact that we always made sure we did a good job, but ventures like those kept Elliot and me in pocket money for years. It was as though people got to know us, got to like us, and got to trust us. Trust travels, and we certainly did well from it back then.

Never judge a person by their tracksuit

To sum up this chapter on the critical importance of recognising and building trust, let me tell you about my first Audi R8. It was one of the dreams that I'd imprinted in my mind and one of the pictures on my wall that kept me focused on achieving success: to own an Audi R8 – I loved the idea of that car.

I went to the local Audi showroom (and I am so tempted to put in print which one – but I won't) to buy the car. Yes, I was actually going to buy it on that day. I had been working 18-hour days for this moment, I had imagined it, I had researched every aspect of the car, I knew exactly what I wanted, the money was in my account, and today was the day I was going to place my order.

Of course, I had also planned to relish the moment for as long as possible, just to make the final trans-action that little more special. So, there I was sitting in the car on the forecourt (a 20-something in a tracksuit), very well aware that the salesman had clocked my presence. As a few more 'potential' customers arrived, all of them in more formal attire than my own, the salesman came over and told me to 'get out', saying that it was not a toy and was for people who were serious about buying one.

Not only did this chap not realise that I was a serious buyer, but he also had no idea that he was already my second choice of showroom. The previous one I'd vis-ited, during the research stage of my purchase, had asked me for a £1000 deposit before letting me test drive the car – even though they were coming with me. I was astonished. Needless to say, neither of these businesses sold me a car that day. My tracksuit and the various hoodies that I feel most comfortable wearing have born witness to dozens of similar stories over the years, but perhaps I'll share more of those in my next book.

Redline Specialist Cars

Eventually, I discovered Redline Specialist Cars, in Harrogate, and these guys have proven themselves to be the epitome of service and respect. My relationship with them started when they agreed to buy my car off me – without even seeing it: now that is the way to engender trust. Since then, every car I have purchased has been through Redline Specialist Cars, and they have never let me down. What's more, I now tell everyone I know about their trustworthiness, their service, their commitment to their customers, and their expertise in supercars. Notice that product knowledge comes last on that list of fine qualities.

The fact is that I would rather deal with a company based a 4-hour drive from me, in Yorkshire, than drive 20 minutes into London – based purely on trust. When people trust you, they will travel to do business with you. They will put themselves out to do business with you. They will go out of their way to encourage others to do business with you. Because good news travels; and trust travels with it.

'Don't worry about the journey, think about how great the story will be.'

Chapter 7

MY WORD IS
MY BOND

The London Stock Exchange is one of the world's original exchange organisations, tracing its origins to the late sixteenth century with traders doing business in coffee shops. Over the decades and centuries, it has changed shape, modernised, and reacted to the activities and dealings of the world's markets. From its early stock and commodities listing entitled 'The Course of the Exchange and Other Things', first published in 1698, to its original rule book in 1812, its role, purpose, and methodologies have continued to evolve.

After a tumultuous and uncertain period during the First World War, the London Stock Exchange was awarded its own coat of arms in 1923, propped up by its centuries-old motto 'My Word Is My Bond' in the traditional Latin form 'Dictum Meum Pactum'. While the motto remains to this day, the practice of taking a trader's verbal promise as a final deal maker seems condemned forever to the history books. In its place, modern technologies (originally developed to shore up and create safety within the markets) have been subject to all kinds of misuse, manipulation, and even foul play.

Interestingly, the practice of open outcry trading remained until the 'big bang' of the 1980s, which saw the formalisation of electronic dealing rather than brokers calling out across the trading floor. This was perhaps the last bastion of traders being taken at their word, rather than the irreversible record of a digital keystroke. I love the (perhaps idealistic and over-romanticise) idea that once upon a time a promise, a look in the eye, and a handshake were all that was needed to secure a transaction.

(The world has, of course, changed. But in my world, and my business, I insist on the principle of 'my word is my bond' still being maintained. Experience has taught me that an honest trader is a good trader and that honesty – outwardly and inwardly – is very good for business).

In general, I am proud of the honour which continues to be displayed throughout 95% of the marketplace. I've had a few run-ins with scammers myself, however, and have even had to fend off those who wanted to pin the label on me and my business over the years. Fortunately, the truth always rises to the surface, and the following story shows you how even an encounter with a despicable man can still lead you to a successful outcome – if you apply the right mindset.

From angry to focused and finding my feet

After my search for high-paid jobs and my efforts to get onboard an oil rig had fallen dead in the water, I stumbled across an advert for a seminar on trading. Elliot my best friend (and now the Chief Operating Officer of Samuel & Co), was busy so I dragged my Dad along for company, and we set off for a London hotel to see if trading was the thing I'd been trying to find.

As I detailed previously, the pictures of yachts, flash cars, a millionaire lifestyle, and an exotic Scottish fishing trip caught me – hook, line, and sinker. I was there for the taking and turned out to be an easy catch.

At the end of his spiel, he offered his 'learn how to live a life like mine' course (usually selling at £5000) for a mere £2000 introductory offer. I still believed him. As I mentioned in an earlier chapter – the only thing that I learned on that two-day course was that I could have learned everything they taught me by searching for it on the internet. The more I learned, the more I felt cheated, and in the days and weeks that followed, I became more and more angry about the 2000-plus (lent to me by my parents) that I had wasted. By then, however, I had become quite adept at channelling anger, and that man's lies drove me to want to become all the things he had claimed to be.

I did meet a couple of good guys during those two days, and we decided that there was more we could do by pooling our resources; then learning, and subsequently trading, together. There were about a dozen of us in the focus group that we set up, and we worked well as a team. I was between leaving college and starting university at this point, and I had a bit more time on my hands than some of the employed members of the group, so my role became research. I would spend hours (often 18 per day) just watching the markets, reading up on the companies we were interested in, and feeding back the information to the others. Eventually, a few of the guys started paying me a monthly fee to take my stock trades – and my reputation began to grow.

For the first few months I was pretty poor, and then I began to deliver a few decent returns. You might be thinking that I was just lucky, got in at the right time, had a gift for spotting a great deal, or really did learn something from the blagger who had taken my parents' savings. But you would be wrong on all counts. I just worked hard, committed long, lonely hours to learning, and was determined to make something good come out of my poor judgement. I was angry, and it helped.

Let me be clear here: my best month came in at 16%, which is pretty impressive if I say so myself, but with such a small starting pot that barely made me £300 before costs. I wasn't amassing enormous wealth in those days, but I was certainly building up knowledge and experience. And the huge amount of time I was spending was a long-term investment which is still paying me dividends to this day.

Back to the seminar and its aftermath. Although I recognised that I had been duped, I was still naive enough to get more involved in this organisation and soon fell further into its manipulative grasp. Looking back, I can see now that as a young guy who was getting to grips with the way things worked, they saw me as something of a trophy to put on display. I guess I was a justification story: if this kid can do it, anyone can. The other thing that is obvious to me now is that the money that organisation was making was through training people, not by trading themselves. The old adage that 'Those who can, do; those who can't, teach' was certainly true in their case. There was a clear pattern of seminar – two-day course – mentoring – then upsell to more training. It was a con; and the sad thing is that the business is still running today (albeit under a different name). Get in touch with anyone in my team, and we'll happily share the name of this company (and any others we are aware of), so you can avoid, avoid, avoid.

I have to stress, however, that other people's bad practice should never get in the way of you working hard, doing the right thing, and enjoying the success that will inevitably follow. If you are reading this today, and you are at the acorn stage of something that you truly love and believe in – please, whatever else you do, keep going. Apply honest graft and proactive learning to what you love doing, and the result will always be genuine wealth (whether that is financial, emotional, or practical).

Who is Samuel Leach?

The other result from me getting involved in the focus group and beginning to hang around with other traders, was that I began to get recognised. I was young, people saw that my trades were successful, and I was happy to volunteer at trader training events as an advisor and helper.

The more people spoke to me, and word got around that my advice had value, the more people were willing to pay for my knowledge. This gave birth to my first entrepreneurial venture within the stock market where I set up a subscription list (eventually comprising around 40 people) who would pay me £30 per month to get the lowdown on my stock watchlist. Alongside the returns on my own meagre trading account, I was soon earning between £1500 and £2000 per month – while I was studying. Mum and Dad got their investment back, and things were looking up.

I soon realised that trading could become a life-changing opportunity. My trading account eventually grew to £2000 and was earning an average of 10%, giving me £200 per month. But I knew, from that day on, that I would one day have a trading account of £200 000 and, at 10%, that £20 000 per month would be a goal worth fighting to win.

Alongside this personal realisation that I could control my destiny, financially and practically, I also saw that I could help others to make their dreams come true and understand their potential. This started with my family and the ways that I could support them but, as time has moved on, it has extended to anyone else who has honest ambition and is prepared to work hard towards their goals.

In my business today, a large part of what we do is teach others how to trade successfully. Yes, I write about my success, post videos about the fruits of my labour (supercars and the like), and I don't hold back from telling people that they can achieve anything they put their heart to – but I am so careful not to sell fake news. You will never see me, or anyone associated with Samuel & Co, promoting lifestyle-selling seminars or pie-in-the-sky pipe dreams. We teach people properly; and we are even prepared to let the right people trade on our trade floor and be around like-minded people.

As my own understanding of the markets developed, and I observed the way that the trading community operated (the good and the bad), I decided that I would do things the right way – I decided I wanted to help.

The key to teaching people to trade is support and mentorship. And, as I said at the beginning of this chapter, to make your word and your promise the bond by which you stand or you fall. You can still be ruthless and take make-or-break decisions, but you must operate within the bounds of what is legally and morally right. If there is one big lesson that I want you to take from this chapter, whoever you are and at whatever stage of your career or life you are, it is that standing up for what is right is as powerful as fighting for what you believe in.

Trust me, there are laws of attraction at work here – and you would be wise to start operating within those laws. My good friend and colleague, Raj, is an excellent example of beliefs and principles being the ideal foundations for a life of wealth and prosperity.

Meet Raj Singh

My future seemed to be mapped out for me from an early age. I grew up working in the family business, a hardware store that they'd owned for 25 years, and from 18 years old I worked in the store for seven days a week. I heard about this seminar on trading and wondered if there might be another, non-DIY, pathway for me to wander along. Later, I learned that Samuel had been in the room that night as well and, like me, blindly handed over my £2000 to be taught a whole load of useless information about trading. Wounded and feeling scammed, I walked away from the course with enough knowledge to start in a small way, but not enough to actually become any good.

Shortly after that, we sold the family business and I started to search out local jobs. There was an advert from this new trading company, Samuel & Co, so I applied and went to the interview. From the first time I met Sam I was massively impressed, and a little bit humbled, that such a young guy could be so capable and full of conviction about where he wanted his business to go. The fact that we'd both been ripped off by the same scammer also helped to make that connection. I enrolled on his course, stayed back late to pick his brain, consistently interrupted him during coffee breaks to ask more questions, and in April 2015 became his first full-time member of staff outside of his family.

I say full-time, we were working out of bedrooms and living rooms back then and communicated online and by phone to make sure we were working to the same goals. Time moves so quickly and so much has happened since that it was only in January 2019, on a company working holiday in Thailand, that we actually got to sit down for 20 minutes to reminisce about the 'old days'.

Since then I've been involved in recruitment for the business, worked on some exciting projects in Birmingham and Madrid, and helped manage the company's social media. Today, I still work on the trading floor and enjoy fighting on the frontline of the markets, while also being part of the algorithm team.

Having seen the company and the people who joined us over the years grow and evolve, from day one, I have realised that everyone is individual and has their own story. People choose to become traders for different reasons, their motivations stretch from family to fun or to fortune, and their personal definitions of prosperity are as diverse as their own backgrounds and stories.

My prosperity algorithm

For me, prosperity means becoming the best version of me (confident, fearless, and capable), but also being financially secure enough to fight the cause of preventing animal cruelty.

It is a passion of mine to stop poaching in all its sickening forms and to support innocent animals whose only crime is to be valuable in the eyes of wicked people.

Since joining Samuel & Co and working with Samuel much of that ambition has already been achieved. I have overcome some of my biggest fears, including talking on stage in front of several hundreds of people, learning to scuba dive (even though I'm scared of water), and starting some charity work. I even turned my dog's Instagram account into a business selling dog food. It was originally Samuel's idea after he noticed that Nico had gained over 20 000 followers.

I've realised that nothing is stopping you doing whatever you want to do in your life. You are your only competition and, if you can find other people who believe in you and associate yourself with like-minded individuals, you really can achieve anything. You just need to be bold, follow great examples, and believe that you will get to your dreams if you keep on going.

As Samuel always says, 'don't worry about the journey, think about how great the story will be'.

'What you do doesn't have to make you rich, it just has to make you happy.'

Chapter 8

FINDING THE YOU-NIQUE IN YOU

In the Robin Williams film, *Dead Poets Society*, there is a pivotal scene where his character, John Keating, has all his students gathered in the school's trophy room. He asks them to go and look closely at the faded, black-and-white year photographs of all the graduates who had studied there decades earlier, suggesting that they'd never looked at them properly before. As they close in, the teacher reminds the boys that they are no different from the young men looking back at them through the shadows of history. He says that they have the same haircuts, are full of the same hormones, feel invincible just like them, and believe that they are destined for great things. He then hits them with a hard truth – that those boys are now fertilising the daffodils.

And then in a moment of true movie magic he says, 'but if you listen really close, you can hear them whisper their legacy to you – seize the day boys – seize the day'.

As I write this chapter, I am 27 years old. To some of you that will seem a distant, almost inconceivable, future. Others, I know, will be thinking, 'Oh, to be 27 again.' If you are the latter, I feel your frustration because at the best-case estimation I am already over a quarter of the way through my life, and there is so much more I still want to achieve. Whatever age you are, I urge you to seize the day, because all of our days are numbered and, like the students in those photographs, everyone has the potential to achieve more with the days they have left (as long as they don't waste their time).

I don't mean to bring a depressing tone to the book, but accepting the fact that you only have a limited time on this planet is one of the greatest motivators to go and use it to the best of your ability. What are you waiting for? Work out what you love and what you are good at – today if possible – and go and pursue it. There is no time to lose.

What you do doesn't have to make you rich, it just has to make you happy. Trust me, material things will not make you happy – living a life that is full of the things that you love doing will. But if you are smart, and if you invest the time to master the rules of the thing you love doing, there is no reason why you can't also find a way to turn the thing you love into a living. (And why shouldn't that be an extremely successful one)?

Who are you?

Wealth is one of those interesting words which can be interpreted in many different ways and means different things to each person. While the most common understanding of the word is probably a financial or material one, its actual meaning is likely to be as individual as you and me. What is universal, especially in most Western societies, is how you achieve wealth – although it is still a barely known secret. The simple truth is that if you can discover the thing in life which gives you the most satisfaction and generates the most happiness for you and the people who you love, you will know what it means to be wealthy. Only you can decide what your something is – because you are unique. After identifying that magical goal, the level of your wealth is determined by how much you desire to gather more of it into your life. The problem most people face is that their effort does not match their desire – or they simply don't believe that the reward will be worth the effort.

This book cannot tell you what form your wealth should take, in the same way that it cannot make you put in the effort to go and seek out that treasure. My intention is simply to help you see that you can; and, hopefully, inspire you to go and try.

Here is a puzzle for you to ponder. I explained in the first chapter how my schooldays turned me into a version of myself that I didn't particularly like, but one that was necessary for me to be able to survive those days. Genetics and circumstance had shaped the unique individual who was born and named Samuel Leach some 16 years earlier. The fact is that everyone reaches this stage of their life, where they have become a product of nature, nurture, and environment. It is the infinite combinations and possibilities of our early lives which create the unique people we become. The puzzle that most people fail even to recognise, let alone solve, is that you can change! Your destiny (genetics and circumstance) is subject to two even more formidable forces – choice and determination.

You were born unique, and you can become the person you wish to become.

Of course, you cannot change your genetics or any physical features (good or bad) about your person. But you can change how and what you do; you can adapt to the environment that you exist within; you can choose your influences; you can become a person who sees opportunities over obstacles; you can decide that you are going to apply yourself to betterment; and you can take action today. It is entirely up to you.

Even if your circumstances today are overwhelmingly restricted and hopeless, I cannot think of many scenarios where you couldn't force even a 1 or 2% improvement.

So, go on, think about it – who are you? Get a piece of paper and start to write down a description of who you are today. Write about the things that you like, what you are good at, if you tend to see things negatively instead of positively, how your friends influence you, if you try harder at some things more than others, what makes you happy, sad, angry, or calm, and if you are satisfied with your life at the moment. Be honest with yourself – no one else need ever see this piece of paper.

Then write down what your ideal life would look like and what sort of person you would like to be in the middle of it. Again, be honest and don't hold back. I love the saying that 'if you reach for the stars, you might just land on the moon', so I always aim high. At the same time, however, if you write on your piece of paper 'living on my own personal luxury island and being waited upon day and night for the rest of my life …', I think you might have missed the point. I want you to think about the sort of things that you enjoy 'doing' and what makes you the happiest.

Trading up your talents

Every single person who has ever been born is unique. Statistically, when you consider the size of the universe, the number of people who have ever lived, the chances of generations of your ancestors meeting one another, and the infinite chances of you being the result of your parents' relationship, you are a living miracle. You may share traits with family members, although you are just as likely to have completely different tastes, but there is only one of you and only ever will be. By default, your uniqueness means there must be things that you enjoy and are good at doing – even if you haven't worked out what they are yet.

Whether you already know what your talents are, or an exercise like the one above has helped you to identify them, you need to understand that pursuing those things is your best chance of living a wealthy and successful life.

For me, I realised that I was good at analysing situations, recognising patterns, seeing opportunities, and using these skills to predict future results and behaviours. I also made a deliberate decision to cultivate my thirst for knowledge, become the best that I could be, and push the boundaries of my willingness to take a calculated risk.

Even as I write this, I can hear some readers thinking: 'That is all very well for you Samuel Leach; YouTube trading expert – but I'm not like you.' Well, I would like to agree with you, but that would make me wrong too. You see, I accept that not everyone has the same natural abilities, but I simply don't accept that people can't put in more effort to change their circumstances, learn a new skill, pursue an opportunity, or turn their own unique talents into wealth. I refuse to believe that some people are so unlucky that they have no skill whatsoever and that great opportunities have never been presented to them.

(As a caveat, I am speaking here in general terms to people living in Westernised countries with the privileges of freedom, education, and stable government).

How to make the change

Everything in life comes down to cause and effect, lead or be led, make choices or go with the flow. For example, if your four closest friends smoke, you will likely become the fifth. If your workmates go to the gym regularly, you will probably end up joining them in the quest for a six-pack. And if the people you hang around with are all budding entrepreneurs, you may well decide that is the life for you too!

Here is the thing though. If you want to quit smoking – get new friends. If you would rather stay unfit than feel under pressure to join in – get another job. And if you hate listening to other people's exciting stories of wealth opportunities, new ventures, defying an hourly rate, and having the freedom to choose your lifestyle, find other places to hang around. You are unique, but you are also mouldable and can be influenced by your surroundings.

I have already told you some of the horror stories of my schooldays and how they influenced my early life. I explained how I retreated to the safety of my bedroom to play war games against invisible foes alongside my invisible friends as a way of escape. The absolute, fundamental, plain-hard-facts of the matter are that if I hadn't decided to do something with my life, I might still be in that room. If I hadn't decided to at least try to get back into college, there would not be around 60 people working for Samuel and Co Trading, also my UK cryptocurrency, Yield Coin, would not exist; my Dad would not have his £128000 dreamboat; and there would not be a Rolls Royce Wraith and Ferrari 488 parked outside my house. I decided to do something and found a way to turn my uniqueness into prosperity and wealth.

Whatever situation you are in today – were born into, have been pushed into, drifted aimlessly into, or are in because of poor decisions you made in the past – you can change your circumstances. It starts with finding out who you are and what you want from however many years you have before you. Then you need to invest in your uniqueness and surround yourself with people or places that support those traits. And finally, you need to work as hard as you can (although if you've found the right thing, it won't really feel like work) until you find your idea of wealth.

Here is an example of how my good friend Chaz did just that.

Meet Chaz Orr

My Mum was a banker and had worked hard to put money into the family home, her retirement fund, some savings for my studies, and a trading portfolio. Then there came a time, with everything feeling safe and secure, that she decided to throw off the stress and toil of the big city and follow her passion into a career change in nursing. So far so good, why shouldn't she do the thing that she loved most of all and help people?

Then came 2008 and the financial crash. Disaster struck, and we lost pretty much everything. Mum was ill at the time (having a major operation), Dad was having an affair (and not paying the mortgage), and I was oblivious to just how bad things were going. Mum's shares (which were 100% tied up in the banking sector) plummeted to a worthless value, by 2011 she had lost the house, and during that time all of her savings had been swallowed up. It was about as bad as it could get and there really was no way to recover the situation. So that was my first taste and lasting impression of the trading world. I didn't trust anybody.

We moved into a rented apartment and, having learned from her own mistakes, my Mum started to teach me how to trade a more diversified portfolio in the stock market. I was interested but sceptical, and basically pretty useless, struggling to get my head around how it all worked. Not deterred, however, Mum moved me on to currency trading (Forex), and after a while, I managed to grasp enough to generate a little success. This was definitely more my thing, and I started to dabble in Forex.

From dabbling to finding my purpose

I ended up going to Hertfordshire University to study Songwriting and Music Production, and between (sometimes during) lectures I'd be trading currencies and trying to keep my small live account in the black. Often I would sit at the very back of the hall or seek out the highest vantage point on campus to try and get enough signal to close a trade.

While on Facebook one day, I noticed that a friend from college, Tom, was talking about trading and mentioned this guy called Samuel Leach. It turned out that he'd been teaching him how to trade and claimed to have made £3000 that week. Far from being impressed, this made me quite suspicious (perfect life, Facebook claims, and all that), even though it was someone I knew and trusted telling me the story. But I did some research and found out as much as I could about Samuel before eventually asking Tom to make an introduction.

I hadn't seen Tom for a while by that time, but what impressed me was the massive change that a few short years wrought on him. From the common old Watford lad, who seemed to be studying just to pass the time, he seemed transformed into a confident, professional, and focused young man with a purpose. Something was going on here – maybe there was more to this than I thought?

Meeting Samuel for the first time put a lot of my fears at ease, but I was still cautious – watching everything your family has worked for disappear does that to you. But his back-story rang true with mine, we'd been to the same college, I felt a good vibe from that first meeting, and Tom was a changed man.

Clarity and big decisions

So I enrolled in the Junior Training Programme (JTP) and committed myself to absorb everything I could about trading, alongside my degree. Of course, that meant a few things had to change about my lifestyle, and an average day began to look a little manic. I'd wake up at 4am, go for a jog, pick up a McDonald breakfast (I know!), return to my room (and cardboard box desk), and start trading – while sneaking off to lectures or fitting in the odd assignment here and there.

This was not easy – my mind was being stretched in different directions, I was always tired, the few friends I had thought I was going crazy, and weekends and weekdays merged into one. But I was making money, loving the learning, and absolutely determined to make the most of the opportunity.

By the end of the second year of my degree, I realised that the education saturation and sleep deprivation was just too much – I had to make a decision. Samuel had helped me see who I was, shown me who I could be, and given me the tools and roadmap to becoming the very best version of that vision. But I still had a burning desire to finish off my degree and get a good result there – I'd worked my whole life towards that goal. After talking it through with him, I realised that I could do both – just not at the same time. I was young and finally in control of my destiny, so I dedicated myself to Songwriting and Music Production for another year (and got a 2:1 for my efforts).

A gap year followed, where I slowly drifted back into poor decisions and financial management. I was spending too much, not clearing my student debt, and generally just letting each day come and go on a whim. The habits I'd been taught all my life were controlling my behaviour again, and it finally dawned on me that I needed to get back into an environment that would bring the best out of me. I knew what to do but wasn't doing it.

To cut a long story short, I spotted a gap in Samuel's armour (yes, he is still learning too) in that his YouTube presence wasn't what it should have been. And I used that opening as a way back into the fold. After a quick conversation, we came up with a plan, and I took over the video production and filming for Samuel's business.

My main goal is to help the world see Samuel the way that I do and learn from the things he does.

Applying the life algorithms, technical training, and mind clarity that I've learned from Samuel has helped me discover my own unique skills and talents. But more importantly, it has shown me that the path destiny had planned for me isn't the one that I had to walk. I have been able to choose a better life and love every minute of it.

'You can be a bad trader forever, but you are only a failed trader when you quit.'

Chapter 9

TAKE RISKS BUT NEVER GAMBLE

There is only one definition that I am aware of under which I could be considered a gambler (and even that is a highly profitable one in which I am 70% more likely to win). The online Oxford Dictionary gives these definitions of the verb, to gamble:

1. play games of chance for money

2. take risky action in the hope of a desired result.

While dictionary.com defines the noun, gamble:

1. any matter or thing involving risk or hazardous uncertainty

2. a venture in a game of chance for stakes, especially for high stakes.

I can tell you with 100% certainty (I'd even put a sizeable stake against it) that I am not a gambler. The only instance in which I am occasionally slotted into a gambling category (and this is UK law, not my own choice or definition) is when I engage in Forex Spread Betting. This is where you bid on the price movement of currency pairs (e.g. US$ vs. £ or € vs. US$). The spread is the difference between the bid and the ask price, and traders will need to evaluate whether the price of the currency pair will be lower than the bid price or higher than the ask price.

Just like any other trade, executed correctly this is a calculated risk – not an uncertain gamble – it is just that the legal terminology deems it gambling. And the result is that the transaction is tax-free (in the UK at least). Happy days!

Risk versus gambling

If you want my definition of a gamble, it is where a trade has odds of 50% or less of turning out in your favour. Personally, I wouldn't even take much below 70% because I want to win, and I don't ever gamble. If that sounds too straight cut and gives you the impression that trading is easy, then think again. You see, the reality is that to be able to accurately calculate those odds, you have to do a whole lot of work and research. There isn't a chart which tells you the chances of you winning a trade – if there was everyone would follow it, and it would defeat itself, by default. It would be a bit like the phenomena created by Google maps and Waze, where everyone follows the 'live data' to avoid the traffic jam and ends up causing another queue in the previously clear road.

The trader that wins most often is the one who has invested more time, effort, and intelligent research into the trade before committing their hand. That is why the trader who takes calculated risks will always (and I absolutely mean always) win over any reasonable length of time. Even if they occasionally lose out on a deal because the unexpected happens. Unexpected, by definition, is not a common occurrence and should be studied to see if any lessons can be learned or simply put behind you as you move on to the next win.

Once again, I hope I am not oversimplifying these things, but the logic is sound – it is the hard work and emotional management aspects of trading that catches most people out.

Risk profiles

In trading, you have different trader profiles. You'll have some whose strategy is to win 50% of the time and others who set out to win 90% of the time. This doesn't make one any worse or better than the other, they have just mapped out different routes to get to the same result: a profit. In simple terms, it means that a trader with a 50% win ratio is likely to win more per trade, while the 90% trader wins smaller amounts per deal but enjoys more fist pumps. Let's look at these in more detail:

Mrs 50% operates on a 2-1 profit factor, meaning that on average she wins twice the amount that she risks. So, for every £10 she trades successfully, she will have a £20 return (in addition to her initial £10).

Mr 90%, however, only enters into deals where he can win half of the amount he has risked. This means that for his £10 to make £20, he must make four successful trades (in effect, winning £5 each time).

Why doesn't Mrs 50% just increase her number of trades, you might ask? Or couldn't Mr 90% copy Mrs 50% in the trades that she makes? Well, that is where people's individual ability (reading the markets and the news, understanding fundamental and technical skills, and sheer volume of effort and research) and risk tolerance comes into play. People who have a low risk tolerance are likely to make poor decisions when under pressure.

I've met traders who quite happily, and very success-fully, operate on a 20% win ratio but regularly see returns of 10 times the amount that they trade. It really comes down to the type of person you are, your skill and experience, and the time you are prepared to invest in analysing the risk.

In Chapter 11 where I teach you Leach Theory, you will meet two incredibly successful people (one a trader and the other one of the most innovative entrepreneurs alive today) who have very different approaches to risk. Ironically, the one who is actually a trader is far less risk-averse than the world-changing pioneer. The following one of his quotes has long been, and will continue to be, the cornerstone of my whole trading philosophy.

'Be fearful when others are greedy and greedy only when others are fearful.'

Warren Buffett

Never take a punt on anything

Why on earth would I, or any sane person for that matter, take a punt on something with their own hard-earned money? To be clear here, I don't count buying raffle tickets to support good causes, or even a few quid a week (no more though) on the lottery, as taking a punt. For most people, these things are a form of entertainment – but there are also a lot of people out there who depend on the billions-to-one chances for their hopes and dreams.

At the very safest end of investing, there are places you can put your money with the same level of certainty that you can be sure your Mum will always love you. For example, if you were to put your savings into certain ETF funds, over 20 years you will get an average of 4% return per year on your investment. I would be 99.9% certain of that – how can that be gambling?

Conversely, I reckon that around 95% of retail traders in the Forex markets consistently make a loss. To most people that would make Forex sound like a pretty risky place to trade. But the fact of the matter is that in the 5% cut of those who make a sizeable profit the same small group of traders consistently appear. So, it must be down to more than just chance.

Let's also consider what the majority of people consider to be the safest place to put their hard-earned sweat-and-tears savings: the bank. Even after the recent crashes and banking scandals, the mindset of the general public is to find the best interest rate they can find and place their money in that account. Now, the truth is that, from a major crash and losing everything point of view, your money is safer now than it was 10 years ago. But the harsh reality is that the interest rates are so low you are actually losing money – or at the very least your money is losing value.

You see, as inflation increases, the actual, real-world, spending power of any particular currency decreases. For example, if Product A is worth £10 today and inflation rises by 5%, it would be worth £10.50 the following year. If £10 had earned 3% in the bank, over the same period, it would now be worth £10.30. That means you would no longer be able to buy the things that you would have been able to buy last year – even though the numeric value of your savings appears to have increased.

Surely, any logic in the world would lead you to the conclusion that savings in low-interest bank accounts are an even worse investment than a gamble – they are sure-fire, 100%, guaranteed loss. Doing nothing is often a bigger risk than taking a punt.

Just to be clear, in case we ever met in person, if there is one thing that makes me shudder it is when a trader says to me that they are going to take a punt on a trade. To me, that just says they are in a gambler's mindset. If you ever say that to me, brace yourself for a lecture (you have been warned).

Trade to win

I assume that you are reading this book because you are interested, to some degree, in becoming a trader or learning more about trading. The single biggest thing I can teach you is to treat your trading as a business. By that I mean you should make business decisions based on what you know of the market. You should do your market (or competitor) research, analyse patterns and past performance, look at outside influences (current or likely to happen), be clear on what you can afford to invest, and have a long-term view.

The difference between a business decision and a personal one is often emotion and mindset. Yes, there is a lot of technical skill involved in becoming a successful trader, but I would confidently say that 90% comes down to attitude, state of mind, and your ability to control your emotions.

If I win 70% of the time, and I take 10 trades, I expect to lose 3 of them. It is easy to get emotional about those losses, but I have worked out the odds, done my analysis in as much as depth as possible, and I expect that to happen. That is simply the way the business works.

Poker is another great example of the general misconceptions around gambling. The odds at casinos, the lottery, one-armed bandits (the clue is in the name), and the like are always heavily weighted against the punter. They have to be because they are run like a business, and a business cannot succeed unless it wins more than it loses. Poker, however, is a player's market. That means that the player's chances of winning, each time they sit down at a table, are almost entirely dependent on their own skill compared to the other players. There is a tiny percentage that depends on the run of the cards or lucky hands, but no more than that – I promise you. You see, the longer the game goes on, the more evenly the chances of everyone receiving good cards becomes because that is a fundamental 'law' (no chance there) of averages. Poker is at least 90% a game of skill!

The very fact that there are professional poker players and a World Championships, where the same top players compete and win year after year, tells you that it is a game which has very little to do with gambling.

You cannot say the same of roulette or fruit machines. In fact, Dale, one of the team here at Samuel & Co, regularly enters top poker competitions and has finished in the top 5 (out of 750 competitors) on many occasions.

I believe there is a way to win on pretty much anything. For me to bet on a horse or the football pools would be gambling, because I am not interested in the form and results of those sports. Instead of going to Ascot for an expensive day out, I would rather take my £500 and invest it in a stock with a track record of returning of 15% per year and that pays out 3–4% per year in dividends. To me, that makes perfect sense.

Take risks patiently

To finish this chapter on taking risks, I want to share with you a principle which will serve you well throughout your trading career. Yes, there are times when you might trade quickly, but that tends to be more the case in the financial markets and Forex trading. With stocks and shares, my advice is always to be patient, make measured unemotional decisions, and base everything on data over gut-feeling.

I have already quoted one of my great distance-mentors earlier in the chapter, but it is so important I am happy to save you turning back the page: 'Be fearful when others are greedy and greedy only when others are fearful' (Warren Buffett). Sometimes you just have to be patient and ride out the storm or the panic. In many ways, the best time to make money in a trading environment is when everyone else is losing their head and chasing their tails.

I have a saying that, 'you can be a bad trader forever, but you are only a failed trader when you quit'. I've seen good traders, bad traders, and quitters. In fact, I've often been tempted to employ, or invest in, some of the persistently bad ones because they have value too: if someone is always losing, I would simply create a reverse algorithm to do exactly the opposite of what they do. That way we'd both make money.

Atish is one of the most level-headed members of my team and is a great example of how a measured approach to risk is a smart approach to prosperity.

Meet Atish Patel

I had been self-employed since I left full-time education and was looking for extra income and part-time side-line opportunities. Through a Google search, I came across Samuel's profile and was impressed, although a little cautious, with what he had achieved at a such a young age. I made an application, although I probably wasn't really that suited and certainly not qualified, but we got on, and the conversation progressed to me joining the JTP.

Within a few months I became a full-time member of the team, and now, four years later, I have the absolute privilege of teaching the programme to others. This involves coaching and ongoing support, and I love seeing other people benefit from the same opportunities that I had been given myself.

My other business is a Sports Bar (the Sakee Bar and Restaurant in Pinner), and that has massively benefited from my involvement in Samuel & Co Trading too. Working with Samuel has opened my eyes to what is actually possible if you approach life with the right mindset and application. Being around like-minded individuals, especially those who are so willing to share their own visions, passions, and positivity, is truly inspiring.

One of the biggest lessons I have learned is to not rely on one source of income. Whether that applies to your trading profile and the number of opportunities you are working on, or to running several businesses at one time, you cannot put all your eggs in one basket. Why would you rely on just one source of income? What if it fails?

Because I have various, totally independent incomes, it simply does not matter to me if one of them is not going too well. Of course, I care enough to attend to the issue and correct it, but because I am not reliant on its income, I have no emotional attachment to it whatsoever. As a result, I can make smart, informed decisions that will fix the problem quicker and more effectively.

Another strong lesson that I drum into students is to learn to manage their expectations. Patience is one of the greatest weapons that a successful trader has at their disposal – that and a good education. Both these things go hand in hand, in many ways, because taking the time to invest in your education takes patience. The fact is that anyone can become a trader! You don't need to learn, you don't need qualifications, you don't need to know how to read charts or study the news; you can just set up an account and trade. It is a massive flaw in the industry and is the cause of much disappointment, heartache, and loss of life savings. It is criminal that people can trade without being qualified.

Human nature is to want everything now – to become a truly successful and prosperous trader takes time. Anyone can achieve that goal if they are prepared to give their all, but it does take time.

'Betty Liu made my day, that morning, and we all made a lot of money.'

Chapter 10

THE
REBELLIOUS
TRADER

So, here is the chapter I've been a little bit nervous about sharing. The reason is that it brings up the subject of ethics and treading the fine line of legality. In the same way that people always say that you should never discuss religion or politics with your work colleagues, ethics is also a subject that you should approach with great caution. The problem is that wherever opinions and emotions mix, there is the potential for taking offence.

For the sake of non-trader readers, it is important that you understand a few basic terms before I reveal any more.

Stocks and shares: the sum of a corporation's shares is described as its stock. The full worth of the corporation stock, as determined by the market's valuation at any given time, is then divided equally among the number of shares that it has issued. This causes individual share values to fluctuate according to the perceived stock value within the market.

Spread betting: this involves speculation on the price movement of a stock or other security. A company will typically quote two prices, the bid and the offer (known as the spread), and traders will make a call based on whether they think the price will be lower than the bid or higher than the offer. This does not involve buying shares; it is just speculation on the price movement. Spread betting is also a way in which trading companies in the UK can go short on a stock, to benefit from the potential fluctuations of the share price over any given period of time.

Penny stocks: (also known as cent stocks in some countries) this is a general term used to describe smaller public companies, where the price per share is very low (i.e. counted in pennies and cents rather than pounds and dollars). Trading in these stocks can be particularly volatile with the potential to make huge losses or gains, and it has historically been the trading ground for many infamous scams.

Incidents and ethics

Here is an example of a short selling incident where a lot of traders made money, and some would question the ethics of how it all happened.

On 2 June 2015, there was a major collision on the Smiler rollercoaster, at Alton Towers in the UK, where several people were seriously injured. Many professional trading companies will pay for professional news and would have heard about this incident pretty much as soon as it happened. A company called Merlin Entertainments owns the Smiler ride, and the educated assumption would be that news of the injuries would soon affect the company's stock value. Experience shows that these sort of one-off 'accident' events tend to generate a fear factor and panic-driven reaction in the marketplace. Understanding this, some traders would have taken a short sell position via spread betting on Merlin Entertainment's shares, banking on the (almost certain) response from the public when the story broke on the evening news. Later that day, or early the next morning, all the retail investors (non-professional traders and trading organisations) with interest in those stocks would panic and sell their shares physically – causing the price to fall rapidly and significantly.

Any trading company (in the short sell position), would then have been able to close their position via their spread betting broker. A lot of people made a lot of money that day.

Here is a circumspect view on the ethics of making money as a result of that incident. It was a business transaction which did not affect the cause or the outcome of the accident. The injured parties were no better or worse off as a result of the trading that was taking place around Merlin Entertainment's stock (in fact, some trading companies will voluntarily give a percentage of their profits from these sorts of trades back to any support funds which are subsequently set up). Finally, while the incident was tragic and could have been avoided, statistically it is a very small proportion of the serious accidents that unavoidably happen each day. For example, in the UK there are an average of 500 people injured in car accidents per day, including 5 fatalities.

For me, a far more unethical practice is blindly investing in steel companies whose production is likely to be used in the production of firearms for terrorism in third world countries. For legal reasons, I am not prepared to mention the names of any of these companies in this book, but the millions of illegal firearms that are killing people every day must come from somewhere.

There are, however, some very public cases of large organizations being found guilty or fined for unethical activities. For example, in 2012, HSBC was fined £1.2bn when it was found guilty of money laundering. Its negligence and 'turning a blind eye' enabled Mexican drug cartels to move dirty money, and it also contravened sanctions so that it could do business with Iran. People might get all 'holier than thou' over spread betting on bad news, but many of them are still happy to bank with HSBC.

Then there was BP's historic oil spillage off the Gulf of Mexico, in 2010. Eleven people were killed in the disaster, the natural habitat was irrevocably damaged, and many people's lives and livelihoods were changed forever. But I doubt there are many people today who still boycott BP service stations, and I wonder if the millions of people who enjoyed the movie (for the sake of cheap entertainment) felt that they were being unethical.

It is easy to point the ethical finger and forget that life is made up of highs and lows, victories and tragedies, which most of us innocently benefit from or fall foul of each day without even knowing.

My own private war on oil

Before I go on, I have to say hand on heart that I never broke the law during my early adventures in the stock market' but looking back, I was often naively unaware that I was dancing fairly close to the line.

In my youthful, idealistic mind, I built up a deep and genuine hatred of dodgy oil companies (based on their ethics, rather than the fact that they had ignored my previous requests to work on their oil rigs). So, in a kind of Robin Hood-inspired vigilante mission, I set about causing them problems wherever possible. On one occasion I nigh on collapsed one of these unscrupulous organizations in one day's trading. (Please note here that not all oil companies operate as these guys did – but I had done my research, and this one's existence was doing no one any favours.)

They were a penny stocks company who were about to go for a re-round of funding. So, a group of my friends bought up a load of their shares individually, to stay below the radar of becoming a major shareholder. But this still created a powerful group of investors within the company. None of us owned more than 4% of the shares and only shareholders with more than 5% in a penny stocks company needed to be declared as such under the law. Without realizing quite how many of my friends were doing this, or how much each other had bought, we ended up owning quite a large chunk of the business.

Because of the volatility of the stock, we gathered on the grapevine that some of the group had made 30–50% profits, so we all decided to sell up to avoid damaging each others' profits. We were also conscious of not wanting to shock the market too much. Some of the group even opened short sell positions, via spread betting, just as others were closing their positions. The large sale of shares resulted in the stock price plummeting, and some of the group came away with some very healthy profits on what was a very good day's trading.

Another time, with another even more crooked oil-based organization, my friends worked their way into a position where they owned over 60% of the shares of the business between them. The company was looking to dilute its share price by about a thousand to one, to raise additional funding. That was clearly not in the shareholder's interest and, discussing it over a pint that night, we all agreed it was an obvious sign of poor financial practices within the company. So, we decided to vote down the decision – as was our right as public shareholders. The next thing we knew, a press release had been issued stating that the majority of shareholders had voted to allow the dilution. Even the maths I had learned under duress at Bushey Hall School told me that a 60% 'no' did not represent a majority 'yes'. So, being diligent and dutiful shareholders, quite a few of the group got on the phone with a tip-off to the FSA.

The whole episode was quickly turning into an ethical nightmare. With the company trying to fix the polling, and then my friends flagging up the situation to the FSA, it opened up a whole can of worms, and loads more nasties soon started creeping out of the woodwork. Ironically, we all lost money on that trade (quite a lot actually), but the fact that that company is no longer in existence today gives me a warm fuzzy feeling. It was a victory of self-sacrifice and giving up a financial reward for the sake of doing the right thing. I can honestly say that I enjoyed that loss immensely.

Just to cover all the bases here, I also know with as much certainty that I possibly can, that any innocent employees who lost their jobs at that company would have easily found work (hopefully with more honest and ethical employers) with other oil companies. Such is the nature of the industry.

And giving to the poor ...

The thing that I think many traders do not realise is that they can be a real influence in the world around them. If you understand the algorithm of how trading works, human reactions, bigger picture intentions, and the power and importance of research, you can make a genuinely positive impact. You can create prosperity for ethical causes, you can generate wealth for yourself and those you love, you can use your own wealth and prosperity to the benefit of others, and you can support and promote companies you believe to be working for the greater good.

My goals are now way beyond simply creating my own lifestyle and looking after the things that good fortune never showered upon my family. I want to inspire others, better educate young people, help people in less fortunate countries than my own, pay my dues (taxes and service) to support the UK government, promote business ethics, and continue to expose and weed out trading scammers. And that is only possible through applying the algorithm of prosperity and continuing to grow and become a better version of Samuel Leach.

Back then, in my rebellious trader days, I did a bit of giving to the poor, too. There was one company, in the green energy sector, which had developed this amazing recycling technology to extract waste heat from a boiler and use it to generate electricity. I know there is a lot more of this going on today, but back then it was the first time I had come across this sort of thing. As much as I was impressed by this company and its green innovation, I was equally surprised at the lack of volume and liquidity in the stock. It seemed that no one in the commercial world cared or would take them seriously. So, I decided to try and give them a boost.

Every time their shares dropped to a low level, I would buy them up, in effect creating a floor in the market to allow them the appearance of financial stability. This meant they would have a consistently stable stock price and market cap from which to keep investing in their technology and growing their business. That company is still trading today, very efficiently and profitably I might add, and they still don't know what I was doing behind the scenes to prop them up – just because I could and because I believed in their vision for a greener energy future.

On another occasion – it still brings a smile to my face thinking of it now – I was sitting in my hotel room in Surrey, overlooking this fabulous golf course, trading on my laptop with Bloomberg News on in the background. There was a little bit of discussion going on with a group of my friends and the stock on another small, but highly ethical, green energy company was moving up rapidly. It hit around 50% on the open market and was already getting very exciting. Then, just to my right from the direction of the TV, Betty

Liu (Bloomberg's glamorous news anchor) said: 'We don't often talk about the penny stocks in the market, but while everything else is in the red there is one stock which is up 50% in pre-market trading.' Betty Liu made my day that morning, and we all made a lot of money.

Settling down and growing up

There are many more stories I could share with you about my early days as a rebellious trader and some of the unconventional, innocent, possibly naive – but always within the boundaries of the system – trades and deals that my friends and I got involved in. As time moved on, however, and I started to employ people to help me grow a business and attempt to change the face of trading from the inside out, we decided to formalise everything.

I could tell you exactly how I turned £2k into £178k, across 12 months, during my first year at university – while still studying for my degree. Then there was the day of my graduation when I was desperately trying to close the biggest single deal of my life, to date, on my phone while receiving my diploma on the stage: £110k richer, my mortarboard flew higher than anyone else's that day, I can tell you. I've had thousands of pounds worth of gold bars sent to me in the post, as thank yous for specific trading tips, just because I once mentioned that I liked them. And, one day, I might even share the details of the one that got away: the £250k deal that I still occasionally wake up in a cold sweat thinking about ...

Today, I am proud to say that Samuel & Co Trading stands out as a beacon of ethics: in the way that we trade, the quality and support that our training programmes deliver, and in the way that we help charities and other great causes in the UK and around the world.

'Achievers are not born great – they just decide to take hold of opportunities and do whatever it takes.'

Chapter 11

LEACH THEORY

People think that mega-successful entrepreneurs like Warren Buffett, Steve Jobs, and Richard Branson are different from ordinary people; that their brains are somehow wired another way. They believe that the great 'first time' pioneers and explorers like Ernest Shackleton, Amelia Earhart, and Neil Armstrong were just born with an intrepid adventuring spirit. And they assume that great thinkers, innovators, and inventors such as Albert Einstein, Nikola Tesla, and Marie Curie were simply gifted with superior intellect. I don't believe any of that is true. And the generalization that I hate most of all is that these brilliant people just got lucky!

Maybe there is a case for genetics and opportunity (to a small degree), but if you really study the lives of the people whose names and achievements decorate our history books, you will discover something more insightful. Greatness leaves clues and identifying those clues will give you a roadmap to follow for yourself. If you look closely enough at successful people's stories, you will see that they all simply dedicated themselves to pursuing their passion with their heart, mind, and strength. They were dedicated to learning as much as they could about their cause, they were prepared to make huge sacrifices to reach it, they embraced being uncomfortable, and nothing on earth would make them slow down or quit their pursuit of greatness.

Steve Jobs once famously said: 'You can't connect the dots looking forward; you can only connect them looking backwards. So, you have to trust that the dots will somehow connect in your future.' My take on this idea is that you only have two choices in life: wait and see where it takes you; or decide (today) that you are going to take charge, apply an algorithm of prosperity, and discover the best version of that destiny.

I believe that everyone who ever achieved greatness did so because they simply realised that they could do better for themselves; they decided to believe and that belief created drive and momentum. (The best thing about this is that you get to decide what 'greatness' means to you. It doesn't have to mean changing the world, becoming a billionaire, or winning a gold medal – it could just mean becoming great at the thing you love doing the most.) My encouragement and challenge to you would be to study great people whom you admire and find a way to align the things that they do with your own unique talents and experiences.

Stealing other people's experiences and philosophies is OK (in fact, I believe most successful people would encourage you to do so and feel honoured that you did). Everyone accepts that life teaches you lessons and you come out stronger if you get through them. Not everyone realises that those lessons can be lost if you don't analyse them and proactively apply them to your life. What even fewer people realise is that learning from other people's victories and mistakes is both faster and less painful than from your own ...

'Leach Theory' is a simple algorithm I developed for creating a set of great people rules. It involves work (reading, studying, observing, and absorbing the wisdom and experiences of others) and discipline, but I promise you it will change your life if you follow the rules.

Leach Theory

One of the most powerful algorithms I have ever created started as a cheeky observation from one of my team. We were talking about some of the successful people who inspired us and how mirroring their mindset, beliefs, and behaviours was a sure way to get the same results. They then said it is almost as if you are leeching the lifeblood out of their success to consume for yourself (an obvious play on my surname) ... but without doing them any harm of course, they quickly added.

Out of that conversation, the term 'Leach Theory' became common around the office and, sometime down the track, we formalised it into a strategic, algorithmic process that anybody can adapt. Try this yourself and, if you follow the steps, it will set you on a path to becoming more like the person who you've always dreamed you could be.

Step 1: Choose wisely

Choose five people whom you either admire, aspire to be like, inspire you, or who have made themselves wealthy (in life or financially). They don't even need to be people whom you like, necessarily, as long as they are successful at what they do. For example, I know that Donald Trump isn't everyone's favourite person, but you cannot deny his brilliance as a businessman, his unyielding determination, and his ability to win over the hearts and minds of millions of people.

I would suggest that at least two of the people you choose should be sector specific – by that I mean they do what you do or would like to be doing. For example, if you see yourself gracing the silver screen, Kate Winslet or Hugh Jackman might be on your list; or if you have your sights set on winning a gold medal one day, Anthony Joshua or Serena Williams would be good people to choose.

Don't stick exclusively to people within the higher echelons of your particular life plan, however, as it is good to mix in at least one person from another field altogether. They don't need to be famous people either, it might be a teacher, an aunt or uncle who has done something remarkable or who inspires you – but they do need to stand out as 'successful' and you do need to know (or be able to find out) a little bit about them and their lives. Your list should be very personal to you and relevant to where you are in your life right now. For example, had I done this exercise 10 or 15 years ago, my list would look very different from the way it looks today.

The other important thing, perhaps the most important rule, is that these people's examples must genuinely mean something to you. It is no good just coming up with people at the drop of a hat – I want you to really think about this before committing to something that might just change your life.

My five people (at the time of writing this book) are:

- Alan Watts

- Warren Buffett

- Steve Jobs

- Elon Musk

- Muhammad Ali.

Now, you choose.

Step 2: Identify their traits

Then, take each of those people and list the things that you like and don't like about them. Despite what I said earlier, most people's lists will comprise their heroes and idols, so they may struggle to pick holes – but it is important to do this if you can because you need to be honest.

To start with, come up with five qualities for each person on your list. You need to write a headline to describe each trait, and an explanation or example of why it personifies their success, attitude, or approach to life.

My list looks like this.

Alan Watts

He was born in England in 1915 and moved to the USA in his early 20s, where he continued his studies into Buddhism and Zen. He wrote around 25 books on religious and spiritual subjects and changed the way people both understood and used Eastern religion for practical purposes.

I have never been into those sorts of things particularly, but from the first time I listened to one of his motivational speeches I was hooked. The mixture of his voice and the common sense that he speaks not only made perfect sense to me but also challenged me and made me start to believe that I could achieve amazing things.

These are the 5 traits (I could easily list 20 or 30) that I most admire in Alan Watts:

1. **Vision:** he believed that our only limitation was that we imagined in our own minds and ambitions – and he proved that this was the truth.

2. **Challenge convention:** he refused to accept that conventional wisdom and ideas were the only way to see things.

3. **Happiness = wealth:** he taught me that wealth meant doing what I enjoyed doing the most (I urge you to stop reading now and Google: 'what if money were no object by Alan Watts' – it will be three minutes well spent, I promise).

4. **Thinking differently:** he was not just a student of the thing he loved, he rewrote the rules of it and defined what it means to think out-of-the-box.

5. **Funny, passionate and well spoken:** I still watch those same videos and speeches today that I listened to 10 years ago because they still inspire me and make me smile.

Warren Buffett

At the time of writing, Warren Buffett is the third wealthiest person in the world with an estimated net worth of over $83 billion, but that is not why I admire him. Like most of the greatest entrepreneurs in the world, he was not born into wealth, nor was he born with an enormous intellect – he simply worked hard, learned as much as he could, and made smart financial decisions. He made his money through investments, which is why I initially took an interest in his story, but it is how he works, his mindset, his understanding of the system, and his desire to give back which really impresses me.

I would also like to add that in 2009, he founded The Giving Pledge, along with Bill Gates, which encourages billionaires to give away at least half of their accumulated wealth to help fund good causes. You see, far from being the root of all evil, the accumulation of personal wealth can make a huge positive difference in the world today.

1. **Self-management:** he actively examines the way he lives (even at 88 years old) and ruthlessly gets rid of anything that he identifies as a bad habit or poor behaviour (things that stop him living a productive life).

2. **Never takes unnecessary risks:** one of the many principles which underpin his success is that he will never risk what he has to get something he doesn't need.

3. **Humility:** he recognises that he is not perfect, so he surrounds himself, and his businesses, with people who are better than him (even at 88, he is still looking to grow and learn).

4. **Capitalise on what you do best:** he taught me that you should stick to what you do best and, if money matters to you, find a way to turn that into financial success.

5. **Do what you love:** it is easy to say of wealthy people like Warren Buffett that they can do what they love because they have financial freedom – but few understand that it was doing what they love which got them there in the first place.

Steve Jobs

If anyone, in modern times, could lay claim to have changed the way that the world works, surely it would be Steve Jobs. Along with his friend, Steve Wozniak, their visionary genius in creating and selling the Apple computer and subsequent i-everything has had a deep and lasting impact on all of our lives.

He was diagnosed with pancreatic cancer in 2003, and the condition tragically took his life (aged 56) in 2011. But in what must have been an incredibly difficult, often painful, and emotionally draining eight years, he still managed to achieve more than most people do in a lifetime. He knew his time was short and he decided that he would not waste one minute of any single day.

1. **Valued time:** he resigned from his position as CEO of Apple just six weeks before he died, citing that he could no longer give the role his full attention – but he continued to work towards his passion of filling the world with innovation throughout those remaining six weeks.

2. **Challenge employees' limits:** not everyone will appreciate this one, but then not everyone is an ideal Apple employee – Jobs loved to push his employees to be the best that they could be.

3. **Follow excellence, not money:** like many entrepreneurs, Steve Jobs went through rough periods where he had no money, but I don't think he ever worried about it – he was focused on the end goal and seeking excellence.

4. **Develop the passion:** he was a great salesman and a passionate persuader, but he famously never sold computers – he sold a way of life and billions of people bought into his passion for it.

5. **Take risks:** taking on the might of Microsoft, IBM, and Dell, from a small start-up business, was never going to be easy and could not have been achieved without being prepared to take significant risks.

Elon Musk

Elon Musk is another example of a man who started with nothing but an insatiable desire to learn and challenge the status quo. Born in South Africa in 1971, and travelling, penniless, to Canada in his teens, he moved in with family members he'd never met and soon began making an impact on the world.

Through all of his ventures – Zip2, X.com, PayPal, Tesla, and SpaceX – he has put his entire faith (and often other people's money alongside all of his own) into ideas that only he truly believed would work. If Steve Jobs changed the modern world, then Elon's ambitions are to change the entire future of the race – to build a super-hotel on Mars before he dies. Wow!

1. **Strong risk tolerance:** I mentioned before that you don't have to like every trait – well I couldn't do what Elon Musk does when it comes to risk, neither would I advise anyone else to – but, boy, do I admire him for his 100% belief and commitment to his cause.

2. **100-hour work week mentality:** Elon recognised from early on in his career that the most precious resource was time – so he used it to pursue his goals instead of letting it drift away into yesterday.

3. **Stand out from the crowd:** the world is full of me-too products and everyone competing for the same space – so Elon always chose to do new things and solve problems people hadn't invented yet.

4. **Feedback loop:** one of the key principles behind his success is the need for giving and receiving feedback so that systems, people, processes, and results can always be improved.

5. **Faith in himself and his team:** the two hardest things about being an entrepreneur are believing in yourself and trusting others to do things as well as you can – Elon has mastered both of these traits.

Muhammad Ali

I have already written about 'the greatest' in an earlier chapter, and he needs little introduction. His legacy and his legend will last for centuries, I'm sure, and he paid for his commitment to his art by suffering from Parkinson's Disease in the latter years of his life – but I don't believe he regretted it for a minute.

As the first person on my list, Alan Watts, once said: 'Better to have a short life full of what you like doing, than a long life that is spent in a miserable way.'

1. **Believe in yourself:** he was the pinnacle of self-belief and famous for his self-promotion – and the fact of the matter is that no one would have bought into the idea of his greatness if he hadn't believed it first.

2. **Imagine your desired future:** today, many sports-people use visualization techniques to help turn their dreams into reality, but Ali was one of the first to do this as part of his training regime.

3. **Preparation is key:** as I mentioned in a previous chapter, his preparation and planning outside of

the ring was the key to him winning inside of the ring – there was nothing left to chance.

4. **Mental strength:** this could be said of any professional boxer because it is a brutal sport – you play football, you even play rugby, but you don't play boxing – but that level of mental strength and resilience is a trait that will serve you well in any area of your life.

5. **Strong, likeable personality:** it can be tough at the top, and you often get a lot of stick just for being successful. Muhammad Ali has taught me that it is possible to be true to yourself, be successful, and still enjoy a good public reputation – perhaps I aspire to that as much as anything.

Step 3: Compare the key characteristics

Next, I want you to go back and compare the characteristics of your five people, looking out for any that match. What you will find is that common themes and ideas will repeat themselves. You might find, for example, that three out of your five role models have a stand out work ethic, or that two of them had to fight through intense discrimination or personal tragedy in their early lives. Maybe it is just the positivity that exudes from them when they speak or their ethics and how they stand up for good causes that attracts you.

Whatever the four or five most commonly occurring characteristics that represent these successful people are, I want you to write them down and sum up each of the ideas in one or two sentences.

1. **Belief (in yourself and others):** the old saying about leading by example is personified in these examples. If you want to create an amazing future for yourself, you will need the help of other people, and if you can't fully believe in your vision, they won't stand a chance.

2. **Do what you love:** someone once said 'if you love what you do, you'll never work a day in your life', and I believe that is a fundamental truth. To do something in life that makes you unhappy makes no sense to me whatsoever and is a sure-fire recipe for failure.

3. **Being different:** basic mathematics tells you that the majority of people, in any given category, are the ones who form the group known as ordinary. So, to stand out as extraordinary, you have no choice but to be different – it is as simple as that.

4. **Taking smart risks:** ironically, two of the people I chose appear to have different approaches to risk. Look below the surface, however, and you will see that they are the same: both study the available information, apply their level of trust in that data, decide what they are prepared to

risk (lose), and then make their commitment. Elon clearly has a higher threshold of risk, so he is prepared to go all in; whereas Warren makes more frequent, smaller, safer trades.

5. **Work ethic:** it takes most people to get into the latter years of their life before the penny drops that life is short and time is precious. When milestone birthdays force you to look back and start counting the years, wondering what you could have done better, it is easy to think it is too late – but it isn't. Today is the best day to start valuing and using your time to do things that increase your wealth (whatever that might mean to you).

Step 4: Make an implementation plan

The final step in Leach Theory is to apply these characteristics in your own life in the form of actions and habits. From each of the commonly identified traits and their summaries, you need to come up with at least one thing that you are going to implement in your life. These mindsets, behaviours, and activities need to be set in stone, measurable, and tangible or you have wasted your time (not to mention an amazing opportunity) in even doing the exercise. If you want your life to change, you need to be prepared to change yourself first.

Incidentally, if you have read this part of the book and not done the exercise (or have no intention of doing the exercise), I would refer you back to the 20% mind-set that I covered in Chapter 1. And if even doing that is too much trouble, I would humbly suggest that you are self-diagnosing a major stumbling block in your route to wealth and prosperity.

1. **Belief (in yourself and others):** continue to listen to, read about, and learn from the people who inspire me – on a daily basis. I know that this will increase my self-belief because it is the same practice that helped build it in the first place. I will then continue in my commitment to influencing others around me (especially my team) and encouraging people to pursue their dreams with belief.

2. **Do what you love:** I love trading, I love teaching, I love being able to help the people I love, and I love seeing other people grow. I work hard, but I can't remember the last time I felt like I was going to work.

3. **Being different:** trading has a reputation for scams and dodgy dealing. I set my stall out to be different and make a stand for honesty, decency, and respect. As a business, we are proactively striving towards these goals and, in the spirit of being different, we are shouting about it everywhere we go.

4. **Taking smart risks:** whether I am using one of the algorithms we have created, trading for the

business, or playing with my own account, I have Samuel Leach's personal set of guiding, unbreakable, and proven rules that I follow. There is a level of risk, but I know that I will always win more than I lose because I follow the rules (the algorithm) that have served me so well over so many years.

5. **Work ethic:** this is simple for me because the truth of the matter is that I no longer 'need' to work 18-hour days to maintain my lifestyle. But I have bigger goals to achieve, and I want to influence more people's lives and change more of the wrongs that I see in the world. To do that I need to put in the hours – there is no other way – so I will continue to work as many 18-hour days as it takes until I am satisfied.

It is over to you now reader. I can only show you what I have done in my life based on what I saw others do in their lives. As I have said before, I do not believe that great achievers are born – rather they just decide to take hold of the opportunities before them and apply whatever it takes to turn them into a success.

You are the only person who can determine your future.

Alan Watts

Vision: he believed that our only limitation was the limitations that we imagined in our own minds and ambitions – and he proved that his was the case

Challenge convention: he refused to accept that conventional wisdom and ideas were the only way to see things

Happiness = wealth: he taught me that wealth meant doing what I enjoyed doing the most (I urge you to stop reading now and Google: "what if money were no object by Alan Watts" – it will be 3-minutes well spent, I promise)

Thinking differently: he was not just a student of the thing he loved, he rewrote the rules of it and defined what it means to think out-of-the-box

Funny, passionate and well-spoken: I still listen to those same videos and speeches today that I listened to ten years ago because they still inspire me and make me smile

Warren Buffett

Self-management: he actively examines the way he lives (even at 88-years old) and ruthlessly gets rid of anything that he identifies as a bad habit or poor behaviour (things that stop him living a productive life)

Never takes unnecessary risks: one of the many principles which underpin his success is that he will never risk what he has to get something he doesn't need

Humility: He recognises that he is not perfect, so he surrounds himself, and his businesses, with people who are better than him (even at 88, he is still looking to grow and learn)

Capitalise on what you do best: he taught me that you should stick to what you do best and, if money matters to you, find a way to turn that into financial success

Do what you love: it is easy to say of wealthy people, like Warren Buffett, that they can do what they love because they have financial freedom – but few understand that it was doing what they love which got them there in the first place

Steve Jobs

Valued time: he resigned from his position as CEO of Apple just six weeks before he died, citing that he could no longer give the role his full attention – but he continued to work towards his passion of filling the world with innovation, throughout those remaining six weeks

Challenge employees' limits: not everyone will appreciate this one, but then not everyone is an ideal Apple employee – Jobs loved to push his employees to be the best that they could be

Follow excellence, not money: like many entrepreneurs, Steve Jobs went through rough periods where he had no money, but I don't think he ever worried about it – he was focused on the end goal and seeking excellence

Develop the passion: he was a great salesman and a passionate persuader, but he famously never sold computers – he sold a way of life and billions of people bought into his passion for it

Take risks: taking on the might of Microsoft, IBM, and Dell, from a small start-up business, was never going to be easy and could not have been achieved without being prepared to take significant risks

Elon Musk

Strong risk tolerance: I mentioned before that you don't have to like every trait – well I couldn't do what Elon Musk does when it comes to risk, neither would I advise anyone else to – but, boy, do I admire him for his 100% belief and commitment to his cause

100-hour work week mentality: Elon recognised from early on in his career, that the most precious resource was time – so he used it to pursue his goals instead of letting it drift away into yesterday

Stand out from the crowd: the world is full of me-too products and everyone competing for the same space – so Elon always chose to do new things and solve problems people hadn't invented yet

Feedback loop: one of the key principles behind his success is the need for giving and receiving feedback so that systems, people, processes and results can always be improved

Faith in himself and his team: the two hardest things about being an entrepreneur is believing in yourself and trusting others to do things as well as you can – Elon has mastered both of these traits

Muhammad Ali

Believe in yourself: he was the pinnacle of self-belief and famous for his self-promotion – and the fact of the matter is that no one would have bought into the idea of his greatness if he hadn't believed it first

Imagine your desired future: today, many sportspeople use visualisation techniques to help turn their dreams into reality, but Ali was one of the first to do this as part of his training regime

Preparation is key: as I mentioned in a previous chapter, his preparation and planning outside of the ring was the key to him winning inside of the ring – there was nothing left to chance

Mental Strength: this could be said of any professional boxer because it is a brutal sport – you play football, you even play rugby, but you don't play boxing – but that level of mental strength and resilience is a trait that will serve you well in any area of your life

Strong, likeable personality: it can be tough at the top, and you often get a lot of stick just for being successful, Muhammad Ali has taught me that it is possible to be true to yourself, be successful and still enjoy a good public reputation – perhaps I aspire to that as much as anything

Samuel's Leach Theory Algorithm

Trait 1	Trait 2	Trait 3	Trait 4	Trait 5
Belief (in yourself and others): The old saying about leading by example is personified in these examples. If you want to create an amazing future for yourself, you will need the help of other people, and if you can't fully believe in your vision, they won't stand a chance.	**Do what you love:** Someone once said: "if you love what you do, you'll never work a day in your life" and I believe that is a fundamental truth. To do something in life that makes you unhappy makes no sense to me whatsoever and is a surefire recipe for failure.	**Being different:** Basic mathematics tells you that the majority of people, in any given category, are the ones who form the group known as ordinary. So, to stand out as extraordinary, you have no choice but to be different – it is as simple as that.	**Taking smart risks:** Ironically, two of the people I chose appear to have different approaches to risk. Look below the surface, however, and you will see that they are the same: both study the available information, apply their level of trust in that data, decide what they are prepared to risk (lose) and then make their commitment. Elon clearly has a higher threshold of risk, so he is prepared to go all in; whereas Warren makes more frequent, smaller, safer trades.	**Work ethic:** It takes most people to get into the latter years of their life before the penny drops that life is short and time is precious. When milestone birthdays force you to look back and start counting the years, wondering what you could have done better, it is easy to think it is too late – but it isn't. Today is the best day to start valuing and using your time doing the things that increase your wealth (whatever that might mean to you).

Action 1	Action 2	Action 3	Action 4	Action 5
Continue to listen to, read about and learn from the people who inspire me – on a daily basis. I know that this will increase my self-belief because it is the same practice which helped build it in the first place. I will then continue in my commitment to influencing others around me (especially my team) and encouraging people to pursue their dreams with belief.	I love trading, I love teaching, I love being able to help the people I love, and I love seeing other people grow. I work hard, but I can't remember the last time I felt like I was going to work.	Trading has a reputation for scams and dodgy dealing. I set my stall out to be different and make a stand for honesty, decency and respect. As a business, we are proactively striving towards these goals and, in the spirit of being different, we are shouting about it everywhere we go.	Whether I am using one of the algorithms we have created, trading for the business or playing with my own account, I have Samuel Leach's personal set of guiding, unbreakable and proven rules that I follow. There is a level of risk, but I know that I will always win more than I lose because I follow the rules (the algorithm) that have served me so well over so many years.	This is simple for me because the truth of the matter is that I no longer 'need' to work 18-hour days to maintain my lifestyle. But I have bigger goals to achieve, and I want to influence more people's lives and change more of the wrongs that I see in the world. To do that I need to put in the hours – there is no other way – so I will continue to work as many 18-hour days as it takes until I am satisfied.

'You have to be prepared to go beyond your own boundaries if you want to grow and become a better version of you.'

Chapter 12

FEELING
UNCOMFORTABLE

One of my favourite emotional states is, ironically, among most other people's least favourite. It is the feeling of being uncomfortable. Just like the words I mentioned in Chapter 6, the concept of being uncomfortable is usually associated with negative things and rarely recognised as the first step towards almost every great achievement in history. For me, that point where I find myself sufficiently far outside of the zone where I feel comfortable is the trigger on the starting pistol. It is the point at which I take the plunge – it is when great things begin to happen.

The dictionary definition of 'uncomfortable' includes descriptions like causing discomfort, distress, pain, or irritation; and being conscious of stress or strain. But here is the thing: precious pearls are formed when an oyster secretes a substance to stop the irritation of a tiny spec of sand in its shell; diamonds are the result of enormous geological pressures; and the naturally occurring performance-enhancing drug 'adrenaline' is released as a result of physical or emotional stress. A positive reaction to an uncomfortable situation almost always generates strength, value, and opportunity. Don't get me wrong here, there are far more examples I could list where pressure, stress, and discomfort cause massive failure, but the key is to apply a 'positive' reaction. Positive participation is the element of this particular algorithm which most people are too afraid to embrace.

Growth lessons from a lobster

I first heard about this lobster analogy while listening to a lecture from a guy called Dr Abraham Twerski, and I realised that he was talking about me. Like all crustaceans, a lobster has a hard exoskeleton which protects all the important soft and mushy parts on the inside. As the creature grows, the hard shell, which is designed to protect it against outside attacks from predators, starts to resist the attempts to expand from the inside. As you can imagine, this growth process begins to make the lobster feel very uncomfortable in its own skin (shell). So, it finds a large rock and crawls underneath the protection of that rock, where it can safely shed its shell and wait until it can grow a new one. Only when its armour is secure again does the lobster venture out into the great ocean and continue living its life beneath the waves.

Have you ever felt uncomfortable in your own skin? Perhaps you've suffered imposter syndrome (where you don't feel you are the right person for the job you are doing). Or maybe you are considering taking a bold step into a new business venture and having second thoughts (for the fourth or fifth time). It could be that a circumstance beyond your control is confronting you and you are on the verge of just running away and hiding under the nearest rock.

Most people, when they feel under pressure or a situation is making them irritable, decide that they are either not cut out for the situation or, worse still, that there is something wrong with them. They give in, run away, break down, or go to the doctor. Now, I'm not suggesting that anyone goes against professional medical advice here, but maybe that feeling of being uncomfortable is actually something else. Could it be that when we are feeling irritable, uncomfortable, or even in pain, that we are simply growing? Could you turn that rock into a temporary state of mind where you pluck up the courage to grow some self-belief and backbone and emerge as a stronger version of you?

In my experience, most people give in too easily. I don't believe anything of significance was ever achieved without someone having to push themselves past being uncomfortable. I'm not just talking about the death-defying bravery of stepping foot on the moon or reaching the summit of Everest. Or even the strength of conviction to stand up to hate, fight human injustice, and change the attitude of entire societies. What about everyday victories and life-changing events, like going to your first interview, asking someone to marry you, learning to drive, or giving birth? You can't tell me that achieving any of these hugely personal growth milestones is in any way comfortable.

Think about every time in your life that you have achieved something which meant something to you. Did it cause any level of pressure, irritation, or discomfort at any time? Was the result worth it? I would even venture to suggest that often the fact that something was hard adds to the sense of achievement and the recognition that we became stronger through the experience. If that is the case, why don't we start to embrace being uncomfortable?

Looking for the uncomfortable

An important part of working out your algorithm for prosperity is to accept that operating outside of your comfort zone for a while is going to be part of the equation. A lot of what I am sharing with you in this book is probably making you feel uncomfortable. I know a lot of people reading it will still be thinking 'it's OK for you Samuel Leach, you have a natural gift for this sort of thing', but that is simply not true. The whole point is that you have got to be prepared to go beyond your own boundaries if you want to grow and become a better version of you. There will be people reading this who are frightened of the idea of investing money or starting their own business or giving up the daily grind to pursue the thing in life that they really love doing. Well, that is great news as far as I'm concerned, because it means that you are close to the edge where you are ready to take the plunge.

I have become so convinced that feeling uncomfortable is the key to personal, business, and emotional growth that I have even started looking for ways to put myself in those positions more often. Let me share one of those stories with you.

Early in 2018, I decided that I would swim the Solent, a 2.5 mile stretch of open water from Ryde on the Isle of Wight to Portsmouth on the UK's south coast. Just to set the scene, I don't like sharks, I don't like deep water, I am not a professional swimmer, and the weekend before two people had died as a result of jellyfish stings just along the coast at Camber Sands. Twenty people had signed up for the swim and when I arrived there were only six of us standing there in our wetsuits, shivering with anticipation even before entering the icy cold waters. It turned out that unseasonably large numbers of mackerel in the waterway meant there were even more sharks than usual (and I hadn't seen the email warning). By this point, I was feeling far more uncomfortable than I was comfortable. Plus, I was the only one of the six without a shark tag (an electronic shark deterrent device).

But I took the plunge because I had prepared, trained, and promised myself that I would complete this challenge. During the swim, the winds and current took us all far off course. At one point I was swimming against the tide for 25 minutes without moving a single body length nearer my destination.

Four of that day's swimmers were pulled from the water due to safety reasons, and only two of us made it to the other side unassisted.

It was a great personal achievement, and it taught me a lot about my physical and mental strength. But the point is that I couldn't have achieved that swim without being uncomfortable. OK, it is not a unique achievement, nor are the half-marathons and other physical challenges that I continue to set myself, but it was something that I had to push myself to complete. Likewise, there is nothing of note I have done in my business life that been easy, or comfortable, but I decided that I would go for it anyway. And more to the point – you can do the same in every area of your life; you just need to get comfortable with feeling uncomfortable.

A practical tool for dealing with discomfort

This is another one of those lessons I learned from someone else. It is part of the algorithm that I use to manage that moment, just before I take the plunge, when the feeling of being uncomfortable is at its peak.

Tim Ferriss, the author of great books such as *The 4-Hour Workweek* and *Tools of Titans,* teaches a technique for dealing with fear by defining the worst-case scenario. I talked about taking calculated decisions and being prepared to lose a few trades to win the majority in Chapter 9. Well, this deals with a similar idea: that occasionally the best analysis and planning in the world isn't enough to predict every outcome. But that doesn't mean you cannot be prepared to deal with every outcome.

Ferriss observed that people often don't start something because they are too focused on the possibility of failure. So, he devised a strategy for dealing with fear. In my mind, it is like the safety net that is there to catch you if you fall after taking the plunge. Let's have a little look at his strategy:

Start by defining the worst-case scenario: the fail. Ask yourself what the result of that would be – emotionally, practically, publicly (how your friends, peers, colleagues, and competitors would view it), and in terms of the effect on your life and business. Next, you make sure you apply every ounce of planning, analysis, strategy, effort, and commitment to making sure you are in the best place to prevent failure. Then you come up with a plan of how to fix the problem if the worst-case scenario happens anyway. Suddenly, the unlikely outcome of you making a complete mess of something that is far more likely to be a huge success looks a lot less frightening. You have a fail-safe plan in place just in case you take the plunge and don't land too well (remember, the odds of success should still be stacked heavily in your favour by now).

Let me share with you a few examples of how I have used this exact strategy in my own life.

Starting a business

At the time when I started my business, I was working at the leading independent private bank in the UK with a reasonable degree of security and a good income. Having worked hard to get there, built up a name for myself, and pushed myself into some pretty uncomfortable places already, I was concerned about my reputation. The thought of losing my salary and bonuses also bothered me, and by then I had firmly decided that an oil rig career was not the one for me.

So, I made sure that I had enough cash behind me to sustain me for six months, I chose the people I wanted to work in the business with me very carefully, and I set up a business model and operational structure that I was convinced would work. I also put my safety net in place by ensuring I left the bank on good terms, with an unlocked door behind me and a way to nudge it open again if I needed to. In other words, I managed my reputation, income, and future before even taking the plunge. It was still an uncomfortable leap, but I knew I couldn't get hurt.

Growing too fast

The day came when I had over 60 contractors working for me and was teaching over 3000 people from across 63 countries. It got to the point where I could walk down the corridor and see people I didn't even recognise and, more concerning, who didn't recognise me. I had no idea if they were any good, if they had embraced the company ethos and vision, or if they would be a long-term asset to the business I was trying to build. It was a little scary, and I felt out of control.

So, I pulled my senior team together and went over the basics of my business vision with each of them again. I wanted them to know the standard I expected from every single member of staff (admin, to researchers, to traders and the management team), and I made sure they knew that I meant it sincerely. Then I asked them to analyse the entire business and feedback the results for me to review. As I waited for their reports, I went back into my office and came up with the repair plan, just in case I didn't like what I heard – and that night I slept well again.

Launching a cryptocurrency

At the time of writing this book, this is happening. It is a few months before Brexit (I had detailed plans for dozens of eventualities there too), and there is enormous financial uncertainty in the air. But I decided that the right 'next step' for my business was to launch our own cryptocurrency. And boy was it a big fat scary decision to take. This, as I'm sure you can imagine, is a high-risk, high-profile, incredibly volatile venture that could either make or break my business and my personal reputation in the global trading world. At times, during the build-up to the launch, I have felt so uncomfortable that it has made me feel physically sick – but I had a plan.

I have done more research than ever before. Read more, studied more, talked to more people, and listened very carefully to the marketplace. I have invested in the best possible team around me and created the correct structure and the right Know Your Customer (KYC) and anti-money-laundering (AML) processes. But what if it fails? Again, at the time of writing everything is going very well, but there is still a great deal of uncertainty in the marketplace. How could I rescue things if they went wrong, recoup my reputation, and recover the losses for my investors so I can pay them back?

I have a plan. It is one I hope I never have to use, but one which will work if it ever has to come into play.

Doing nothing is often the biggest risk of all.

Taking the plunge and coming up wealthy

I never take a punt on a trade. I simply refuse to risk losing money I have worked so hard to earn. But I'm always prepared to take a plunge into the right pool. Think about it. Would you dive head first into a pool without first checking how deep it was, if there were rocks just below the surface, if it was infested with piranha fish, or even asking if there was any benefit to taking the plunge? I hope you wouldn't. But, if you'd discovered there was nothing but a bag of gold down there, it was safe to jump, and all you had to do was hold your breath for 10 seconds while you attach your flag to it to claim the prize, you might think it was worth getting wet.

Successful trading is just like that. It is a case of doing your research (the more thoroughly you do this, the better) and making wise decisions where the odds of success are significantly in your favour. And, if you are really smart, you should search out more than one promising pool to dive into, just in case your information was wrong or there was not as much gold in the bag as you'd hoped.

Conclusion: Finding your algorithm

Like any younger brother, I idolised my older sibling. Growing up, James was always faster than me, stronger than me, allowed to do things that I wasn't allowed to do, and his quiet assurance was something I aspired to match. What I didn't realise was that his Bushey Hall School experience was having a very different impact on his life than it would have on mine. It is obvious to me now why he left that school on another path to the one I would later find myself on – because he entered the school as James and me as Samuel. He was always my older brother and we came from the same stock with the same parents – but we could scarcely have been born less alike.

Meet James Leach

Samuel was always quite headstrong and wanted to do things his way. It was clear from an early age that he did not really respond well to convention or being told what to do. To me he was hyperactive, often rebellious and, while he was my little brother who I would have done anything to protect, we really didn't have too much in common. The old expression 'chalk and cheese' springs to mind, in that we looked similar, but that is where the resemblance ended.

By the time Samuel had been through school and college and started to find his forte in the trading game, I had joined the police and then the Counter Terrorism Armed Response Unit. It would be something of an understatement to say that we were two brothers living very different lives. Perhaps the only similarity in our day-to-day activities was that we both learned to keep a very keen eye on managing risk.

The concept of having a career for life is now an old-fashioned one, and even if people do the same thing throughout their career, it is rarely with the same company nowadays. But in the police, it is almost a given that you will proudly wear the blue and keep the badge through to retirement. And in my head, that was the route I was on – I'd invested too much time, effort, commitment, sweat, and blood to think of doing anything else. I also had a young family to think of and, while I certainly didn't see them as often as I wanted to, I was happy that they had the security of my, not insignificant (life-on-the-line), police salary.

By 2018, I was on level six of the seven-scale pay scheme and doing OK. But one day, talking to Samuel, something made me wonder if there was another way to live and give my family the financial security they needed as well as more of my quality time. And in September of that year, I decided that the risk was all in my favour.

Swapping one risk for another

Everything in life is a risk. From crossing the road to paying for a takeaway online – there is always the possibility that you could lose your life or lose money. By joining Samuel & Co Trading, I gave up a career that I had worked all my life to excel at. The fact is that I could return within two years, but I would have to go through all my basic and advanced training again and potentially start on a lower pay scale. It is a risk.

On the other hand, I get to spend more time at home with my family and my life expectancy has increased significantly (which they always worried about more than me, to be fair). My income has also already increased and I have quickly learned that being exposed to the Samuel & Co environment certainly opens your eyes to potential and opportunity. All my life I have been taught to make split-second decisions, analyse life-and-death scenarios, and obey strict rules and methodology – while also thinking out of the box. And all of that had to be done in an analytical, non-emotional way.

One of the things that Samuel has shown me is that my experience is perfect for becoming successful in the world of trading. The point here is that if I, a Counter Terrorism Armed Response Officer, can change my life and do something completely different in the world of trading – surely anyone can.

The Traders' Challenge

It wasn't necessarily James joining the business which prompted the idea of The Traders' Challenge; it may have had more to do with shows like 'Who Dares Wins – are you tough enough?' where civilians are put through SAS basic training to see if they can make the grade. But I have always had the idea in my head that I would like to take someone off the street, or a person with seemingly no life prospects or hope of a break, and teach them to trade.

The idea behind this book is basically that anyone can find and achieve prosperity. It is as simple as working out who you are, what you love doing, and what you are good at doing (those two things are invariably the same). Then finding some way to learn all that you can about that thing and applying yourself to practice and to become the very best that you can be. In following this simple formula, everyone can be happy and successful. And, once you have become an expert, you should be able to find a way to monetise your skill – if that is indeed what you want; you might not be remotely interested in financial wealth, and that is fine too.

The algorithm part of the process is simply that you can represent your vision, desire, activity, and progress as a system that you follow. The structure is there, as described throughout this book, and the variable, which ultimately determines the result, is the amount of effort and commitment that you are prepared to apply.

To test this theory, I launched The Traders' Challenge early in 2019. We took 18 people, from all walks of life, stuck them in a room and started to talk to them about trading. Among the group, we had ex-military personnel, a market stall trader, a teacher, some students, a supermarket cashier, and a recovering drug addict who had spent years living on the street. At the time of writing this book, we are halfway through filming, and nine of the candidates are left in the process. It has been fascinating to watch them learn, grow, and discover their own potential for prosperity.

At the end of the show, anyone who proves that they have what it takes will be offered a job role with Samuel and Co Trading. If they can do it – why not you?

Finding your algorithm

Everyone is different, I get that, and some are born into more favourable circumstances than others – I get that too. But what is stopping you from becoming more prosperous? I was born into an ordinary home, in the ordinary town of Watford, and was destined for a life of ordinariness. Along the way I dealt with a tough school life which turned me into an angry, rebellious teenager; I hid in my bedroom for a year to escape life's reality; and I never displayed any obvious signs that I knew how to learn. But I worked out my algorithm – I worked out what made me tick – and I worked out how to turn it into prosperity.

If I can do it, then so can you. I refuse to accept that you, reading this book now, cannot go and become a better version of who you are now. Imagine who you would like to be, picture the people who inspire you, go back to Chapter 11 and apply Leach Theory, do whatever it takes! You only have one life, time is ticking, and you have the algorithm of life and prosperity in the palm of your hands. Go and become somebody amazing. Go and become a more prosperous version of 'you' today.

To get started in trading or to follow my ongoing story, please connect with me through my social media channels:

- Instagram: samuelleach

- YouTube: samuelleach

- Website: www.samuelandcotrading.com

I would love to hear from my readers and learn how you have unlocked your algorithm of prosperity and success.

Index